Caring Grandparents

Part 1 - Grandparents Caring **ABOUT** Grandchildren

&

Part 2 - Grandparents Caring **FOR** Grandchildren

Neil Taft

Neil Taft

Mission Statement

The mission here is to add value to your considerable intention **about** and **for** your Grandchildren through additional knowledge and support of your efforts as a Grandparent. There is power in numbers and knowledge. This book will let you know that you are not alone and, at the same time, share what other Grandparents are experiencing.

Neil Taft

Table of Contents

PART 1   Grandparents Caring ABOUT Grandchildren

INTRODUCTION 1

1. OUR ROLE 13

2. EARLY ON... 30

3. THE EXTENDED FAMILY 40

4. CONNECTION TO YOUR GRANDCHILDREN................................ 49

5. OUR LEGACY 68

6. RESTRICTIONS AND ALIENATION 76

7. SUMMARY OF CARING ABOUT YOUR GRANDCHILDREN 87

8. RESOURCES 89

PART 2   Grandparents Caring FOR Grandchildren

1. STEPPING UP 94

2. THE THREE D's – Drugs, Desertion, and Detention 113

3. PRACTICAL CONSIDERATIONS 118

4. RESOURCES 123

INTRODUCTION

Let me begin by offering you a glimpse into WHY I wrote this book. It can best be illustrated by the following story.

It was a Saturday afternoon, and I was sitting at my computer writing this book on Grandparenting. I was writing about how I had committed to sending each of my Grandchildren what I call an "Electronic Hug" at least once a week. I stopped typing and grabbed my phone. I always start with my first-born Grandchild, Zak. He is 35 years old and lives about 6 hours away.

We messaged back and forth as follows:

Me: "While writing my Grandparenting book it brought back fond memories of hanging out with you. I was recalling our Helicopter ride (a first for both of us), along with Monster Trucks and race cars. I think there is a theme of motors here. Hope you are doing well."

His reply came swiftly:

ZAK: "Very well, I'm actually taking Little Dionte (my nephew) to go see some Monster Trucks tomorrow! I'm not sure who is more excited, me or him! (smiley face emoji)

Me: "The apple doesn't fall far from the tree."

Here comes the amazing payoff for this Ole Grandpa.

ZAK: "I think about those same memories with you all the time too. I was just telling someone yesterday about our first ride in an airplane when we went to Chimney Rock. All those times we went and raced Go-Karts. I still have my signed photo of Jeff Gordon that you got me too....and my Mom's signed photo of Harry Gant on a motorcycle! (I'm assuming that one came from you as well). I'm not sure I've ever officially thanked you for all the great times we've had. But genuinely, they meant more than you'll ever know. I didn't have a lot of great memories with anyone as a kid. Pretty much all of those came from you. Best of all, I learned from you how to pass that same gift down to other kids and try my best to be that person for every kid I can. So seriously, THANK YOU!!! I love you, Grandpa."

Me: "Love you back."

This book is about stories like this and many more from Grandparents that Care about their Grandchildren. I truly believe that being a Grandparent is a noble and sacred mission for the mature heart. To honor this mission, I offer the following promise. In this book if a choice is presented between telling you what you want to hear and what is the best for our Grandchildren I apologize in advance because their best interest is paramount.

Since you will be a Grandparent for twice as long as you will be a parent you will understand that I wish I had a book like this 35 years ago. Not only do I wish I had this book or one like it, I wish I had the knowledge and network of other Grandparents to help me know that I am not alone in my quest. Now you can know that you are not alone.

So many Grandparents think they are the only ones going through some of this stuff that happens in their families. When we reach back for guidance from our own experiences, we realize that those experiences come from a completely different time and a completely different extended family structure. Support and affirmation come from hearing what other Caring Grandparents are going through.

Our Grandparenting experiences are so varied, and they change as our families and our Grandchildren grow. They become more complex with each addition to our extended families. The entire landscape for Grandparenting has changed significantly as our world evolves. We find ourselves living further away from our Grandchildren. We are searching for ways to stay connected over these long distances. We find that almost all of our means of communication have changed. Some in ways we can harness but they all feel so foreign to us. We find that our Grandchildren are exposed to so much more at an ever-younger age than we were. This makes meeting them where they are so much more difficult. We find ourselves challenged in some unsettling ways but yet we are motivated by our Love for these little miracles to find answers.

What you are about to read is a Grandfather's philosophy of More Love for our Grandchildren and an affirming way to partner with their parents. There exist forces that can cause us to be challenged in this quest and that is what this book aims to educate you about, prevent where possible and/or help you with. I advocate for an approach of Both/and instead of either/or. I believe this is done through knowledge and thoughtfulness motivated by good intentions. I have to believe that there is a better way to approach what is becoming a drift of familial separateness and steer, instead, toward more inclusion for Grandparents. I am dedicated to sharing the findings of my research for these past 20+ years so you can understand that others have walked this path that can lead to becoming an even better Caring Grandparent. The benefit is that we add value to ourselves, the entire extended family but especially to our deserving Grandchildren. I don't believe we live in a zero-sum world, especially when it comes to our Grandchildren. I do, however, recognize that the onus has fallen more on the

Grandparents shoulders to find ways to bridge the generations and new societal norms of family dynamics. Most of us Grandparents have had to say, in one form or the other, to our kids and Grandkids that life is not fair. It may be time for us to apply this truism to our own plight in the journey of trying to navigate this thing called extended family. I personally abhor wasted energy, in this case wishing it wasn't so is just that. This journey is not about what is fair but rather about what is effective. Based on that it is important that we approach Grandparenting from a strategic rather than a fairness focal thrust.

Knowledge and shared experience are antidotes to a lot of what concerns us as Caring Grandparents. This knowledge will enhance your Lasting Meaningful Connections with each of your Grandchildren. Your newfound observations can also help you avoid some of the most common potholes on this road to where you would like to be. A bonus is that avoiding these potholes enhances the entire family while adding a ton of value to our Grandchildren.

At a recent author's retreat I was being interviewed by Jack Canfield, Co-author of the Chicken Soup for the Soul series and a Grandfather to a 10- and 2-year-old Grandchild. His question to me was,

"Neil, what do you find is one of the most common misperceptions that Grandparents have?"

My answer was, "Grandparents often think that Grandparenting will come naturally. Some think it is kind of like falling off a log." That may be true for some very small minority of Grandparents but for the rest of us you should know that learning and intentionality are the key to success with our Grandchildren.

Like life in general, there are no free lunches when it comes to quality connections with our Grandkids. There is, however, a tremendous amount of Joy to be had but it only follows our paying close attention, meeting our Grandchildren where they are and applying our own brand of Intentional Love and Caring."

I should add a caveat to that statement, we will be well served to meet not only our Grandchildren but everyone in our extended family, especially the parents, where they are and let go of this notion of where we wish they would be. Much of this book deals with just that idea and the consequences of ignoring this pearl of wisdom.

This is a good place to be clear about the best of the best practices. Letting the parents become parents takes more Love and consideration than you first thought. I will go so far as to say that it is existential to you having Lasting Meaningful Connections with your Grandchildren. Read on and you will understand that statement much better. To supercharge this best of best practices let me suggest that when it comes to partnering with the parents you will do well to find ways to add affirmation to your support for them. Lest you forget, parenting is not a walk in the park.

My mission is to share information and stories about what is working as well as what is not working for me and other Grandparents in today's family environment. Stories and information from a huge cross section of Grandparents and affirmed by the experts in this field will be instructive and valuable as examples that most of us can relate to and adjust the circumstances to apply these insights to our own families.

It would be understandable for you to wonder who this guy, Grandpa Neil, is and why you should listen to him? Fair enough.

I am a 79-year-old Great-Great Grandfather with 6 Grandchildren, 5 Great grandchildren and Hallelujah! one Great-Great Grandchild, Kingston. In addition, I have become a quasi-Dad and Grandfather to several families that have hitched their wagons to our, very inclusive, family over the years. This is my fourth Grandparenting book. Over the past 20+ years I have hosted and shared information on two websites (CaringGrandparents.com and more recently on GoodtoGreatGrandparenting.com), I am a retired Youth Minister, Public Speaker and a lifelong Youth Advocate. However, all of those accomplishments pale in comparison to my greatest achievement.... **All of my grown children and Grandchildren still enjoy my company on a regular basis.**

In an effort to make this book as meaningful as possible for you the reader I have separated this one into two sections. Part 1 is written to share the best practices and experiences to help you ignite your own imagination as to how you can best care **ABOUT** your Grandchildren. Part 2 is filled with information on how you can best care **FOR** your Grandchildren in the event you become one of the Grandparent households that are raising over 8 million Grandchildren. You will be given a behind the scenes look into families that find themselves, often reluctantly, drawn into this situation.

FYI: Part one relates many stories of how these Grandparents got to the tragic situation and my hope is that a possible downward spiral can be interrupted before it devolves into Grandparents having to rescue their Grandchildren. Seems unlikely? 2.5 million Grandparent households are raising their Grandchildren. That is a real number.

You will realize that Grandparenting is not a spectator sport! In these pages you will learn, from experts as well as the experience of others, those things necessary to be a Grandparent at your highest and best level.

These pages contain information about:

- How to unleash your Grandparenting Superpower

- Becoming a New Grandparent

- The importance of partnering with the parents

- Navigate the tricky waters of an extended family

- Communicate effectively across generations

- How to prevent Alienation

- Best practices for Long distance Grandparenting

- Becoming more effective if you are a Grandparent raising their Grandchildren.

- Finding the best resources available to help you in your situation

This journey to enjoying Lasting Meaningful Connections with your Grandchildren actually begins way BEFORE the birth of your first Grandchild. Due to the complexities of extended family dynamics, setting the tone for success in the entire family requires a considerable amount of understanding, communications and more understanding. Intention is not enough. This is a highly charged time in your family that is packed with possibilities and potential pitfalls. Everyone will be best served by a large dose of thoughtfulness and consideration. Chapter Two of this book raises some of those "opportunities" to prevent unintended resentments and misperceived slights that could resurface as time marches on. Every solid, long-lasting structure as well as relationship is built upon a solid foundation.

Every extended family is composed of varying personalities and folks bound together by unique bonds. If we consider the diverse selection processes that bring this extended family together and then add to that the goal of finding a way to make this arrangement as functional as possible, we may come pretty close to defining our challenges. These pages contain stories of how this can happen in your extended family with an eye toward preemptively avoiding some of the pitfalls as well as dealing with the inevitable conflicts.

Our overarching goal is to create and maintain Lasting Meaningful Connections with our Grandchildren by partnering with their parents to make this possible. This part of the journey seems logical but requires some knowledge and lots of communications flavored with some adjustment of expectations. Most of Part 1 is dedicated to just this endeavor. Much can be learned from the experiences and stories of other Grandparents. Those lessons can then be adjusted to fit your circumstances and help prevent misguided actions on our part. Most of us enjoy some pretty smooth relationships with our families and extended families. This does not necessarily mean that this fair weather will continue on its own.

In some cases, despite all your efforts, circumstances don't play out in your favor, and you wind up in a defensive posture rather than a proactive role. With a divorce rate hovering around 50% it will be helpful for you to know some of the stories of Grandparents that have been unjustly restricted or prevented from having time with their Grandkids. While the book initially deals with ways of preventing just this, eventually, we are faced with the complexity of some family members that don't see the importance of our Love for our Grandchildren and the role it plays in their growth and development. There are ways of interacting with all concerned that can improve your chances of avoiding bad outcomes. Keep in mind that as long as there is any hope of influencing the outcome there are things you can do, even, as an alienated or restricted Grandparent that can improve the circumstances and/or soften the blow.

I have counseled with and received a lot of messages from Grandparents filled with sadness and guilt about being cut off from their Grandchildren. In the resources I will offer some hope to soften the sadness, some stories to offer support during trying times and some potential and seemingly miraculous solutions that have worked for other Grandparents. Also, in the resources you will find some valuable and hopeful information from organizations like Grandparents Academy and other experts about reconciliation, etc.

When it comes to the guilty part of this I have a lot to offer. First you may want to grant yourself some Grace when it comes to feeling guilty. There have been some significant societal changes that have increased the incidence of Grandparent estrangement that go beyond the scope of what I can offer in this book. There is a reference in resources to Dr. Joshua Coleman and Rachael Haack if you are interested in a perspective of how we got here. The other caveat I can offer is that this whole extended family thing has its own set of challenges, some of which are beyond your control.

Speaking of what is in your control there are a ton of best practices that if you are willing to learn and implement them, they will increase your chances of avoiding estrangement.

I included Part 2 of this book just in case you find yourself among these 2.5 million Grandparent households that are suddenly thrust back into the responsibilities of parenting your Grandchildren. You will need a lot of resources and support to weather this storm. I think that because the numbers have grown so large there are finally a growing number of resources for these unwitting participants that, after some family disaster, are faced with a daunting task. The stories surrounding these, now millions of, Grandparents are complicated and sad but I have included them because they are also instructive. My hope is that you can find at least some comfort in knowing that there are heroic Grandparents in every community that have stepped up to save their Grandchildren in a time of great need and the results are rescued Grandchildren that thrive. If you are blessed, as I am, use your privilege to help those that are going through this darkness. Raising awareness, volunteering, befriending and supporting someone you know that is facing this dilemma or donating to some of the many groups that support these brave Grandparents. One of the oft overlooked ramifications of Grandparents that are now raising their Grandchildren is that they become socially isolated. Their circumstances suddenly change but their social circles are geared toward adult communities. This is an area where you can offer the most support. Continue to be a friend to these brave folks.

We all crave a fully functioning, Loving extended family. While some exist, they are few and far between, even the ones that exist still require all the efforts and perseverance included in this book to sustain such a family. The norm is that most branches of the family are functioning pretty well but there is, in the case of Grandparents having to raise their Grandkids, part of that family that requires rescue and/or at least special attention. It is not hyperbole to call this a quiet, yet little known crisis with enormous consequences for millions of Grandparents and Grandchildren. These enormous consequences manifest themselves in many ways and for many generations.

There are all kinds of considerations when a well-planned life of Grandparents is derailed by the needs of their Grandchildren and the dysfunction of their own child. These range from disappointment to extreme stresses on the Grandparents. I included this section to raise awareness and to serve the considerable needs of these dedicated, yet unwitting Grandparents. There are a lot of resources that are directed to help in this area. Some of the resources are for the sake of the children but more importantly there are much needed resources for the Grandparents. Having to step up and accept this responsibility is fraught with challenges that few are prepared for. Your intention will get you in the game but there is soooooo much to consider for the long run. Your hopes and dreams have been derailed and your life will change forever. If this crisis visits you, these are no longer your Grandchildren, You are now "stepparents at 60". Anyone who has been one, or knows, a stepparent will recognize the challenges of this task. Add to that the often-deep emotional wounds of you and the

Grandkids. It will begin to become clear that significant challenges are ahead. You will also begin to sense the magnitude of the situation. This will create stresses you can't even imagine at the outset. My hope is that if you find yourself in this situation that you will avail yourself of as many of the available services as are necessary and don't wait until things get bad, begin early. This is one case where it does take a village.

Finally, at the end of each part of this book you will find a list of some of the best resources available in any given circumstances of Grandparenting, especially for Grandparents raising their Grandkids. These are my friends, thought leaders and top experts in this field of Grandparenting who care about the future of our Grandkids.

If I had to pick a starting point for Part 1 it would be partnering with the parents and Part 2 if you are a Grandparent raising your Grandkids, I would suggest starting with support groups. These are like-minded people who are now going through some of the same things you are, or they have gone down some of the same roads you will be traveling. I hope this helps.

I sincerely Thank YOU for being a Caring Grandparent. Grandpa Neil

PART 1

Grandparents Caring ABOUT Grandchildren

Chapter 1

OUR ROLE

"I am a Grandma, what is your Superpower?"

Author unknown

There is a lot of talk of Superpowers going around. Becoming a Grandparent doesn't automatically pin that badge on you. Becoming a Caring Grandparent will get you nominated. As an active, Caring Grandparent you will probably be "Crowned" with some kind of nickname such as Gramps, Grammy, Nanna, Poppa, etc. Some of these monikers come from the Grandparents themselves as preferred nicknames, some are suggested to differentiate each of the Grandparents, but wait, when your Grandchild begins to speak, they may put a valued, albeit mangled pronunciation on your nickname. It is at that point that some of our most unusual and cherished nicknames originate. I have heard of Gammy, Umpa, etc.

Regardless of your title, you as a Grandparent hold a position of honor and unlimited potential to be a force for good in your Grandchild's future as well as for the entire family. When executed at its highest level it can become a sacred role. This is not hyperbole, if you go all in it can become a noble and extremely valuable calling. This opportunity and your position is unique in this universe and it is in your hands to maximize your influence. The more intentionality you add to the process the closer you get to Superpower status. This entire book is about how Super you intend to become, the process for accomplishing your level of Superpower that you choose to attain and all of the benefits to you, your Grandkids and ultimately your entire family. The seatbelt sign has been illuminated so fasten that belt, sit back and enjoy your flight.

Your choice to become a truly Caring Grandparent will be rewarded with immense Joy and probably some immense frustration. In most families this is the way it plays out. You are about to read story after story that illustrates that even grit-your-teeth good intentions may not be enough. You will be called upon from time to time to suffer some awful and illogical trials because of circumstances beyond your control. To set the stage for what you are about to read I wish to make clear that I fully understand the frustrations of good intentions that fail to hit the mark mostly because of other players in the family. I also recognize the sheer Joy to be derived from attaining these Lasting Meaningful Connections with your Grandchildren. As you will learn in this book, there are approaches to these circumstances that greatly enhance your odds of better outcomes. The only behavior you can control is your own but with good intention and a lot of effort you stand a good chance of influencing a better outcome in your family.

Families tend to fall somewhere on the spectrum. In some families there are as many spectrums as there are extended family members. I will be introducing you to a variety of Grandparents and their circumstances. Some have added a dose of new knowledge and consideration to their intentions and consequently they come much closer to hitting the mark they are hoping for. Some are completely cut off from their Grandkids and most are in the middle of the spectrum wanting things to improve. I can't imagine anyone who has purchased this book and has read this far in that is not doing their level best to be the most Caring Grandparent possible. It is for you and to this end that I share these stories and this information.

To be sure that we have the right mindset to approach becoming our best Grandparenting selves, it is helpful to keep in mind this thought; "Life is complicated. Family life is a multiple of complicated and extended family life is exponentially complicated." It is with this in mind that we will have to stay laser focused on the best interest of each and all of our Grandchildren. The task is clear, the path is fraught with obstacles, but we are the only ones equipped to deliver on what is rightfully due to our Grandkids. Grandparent Power is a force that is hard to deny. Intentional Grandparenting with a purpose is a force Du jour.

One of the things most of us are not very good at is dealing with conflict. Bad News! This is an extended family and over time there will be conflict. Most of this conflict is out of your hands. Or is it? One crucial time to be intentional is when there is conflict. If you're trying to create a Lasting Meaningful Connection with your Grandkids, you have to keep their interests top of mind. When conflict arises you DO have choices, some choices are hard, and others are even harder to affect. All, and I mean ALL my research points to this being a defining moment for Grandparents, especially. The normal family response is that everyone chooses up sides and…………….what? What happens when we choose up sides, it becomes a contest. In a contest there is a winner and a loser. What if? What if we keep our goal and Grandchildren in mind and sit this one out. What if we make our decisions based on long term strategy instead of emotions? What if we shift from being on the problem side to being on the solution side of the conflict. Remember this wisdom from Dr. Sue Cornbluth (A conflict resolution expert); She states that "Conflict cannot be resolved by more conflict."

When conflict arises, this may be one of the most powerful tools in your toolbox. The research is clear, the examples are many that there are folks who have to be right all the time. If I have heard this once I have heard it a dozen times, "Well it has worked for me in the past." I tell people that Grandparents, like all people, have the right to be right. However, **how much do they want to pay to be right?** That is really the question they should be asking." When you pause and consider that idea, it may come in handy in all kinds of human interactions. My experience of the past eight decades is that it is not so much your need to be right but rather your need to make others around you wrong that lights the fire of trouble.

It may just be a matter of your timing in stating your "need to be right" or the way it is delivered. It may also be that it is not as important to state it as it is to have more valuable time with your Grandkids. This is exactly what this and my previous books are about. When conflict comes up, and it will, you have to keep the best interest of the Grandchildren top of mind. One very prominent and learned Grandma suggests that you have a metaphorical piece of duct tape in your pocket or purse to place over your mouth at times like these. Remember, unattended resentment is cumulative. The sad thing is that when it comes to extended family resentment it is often born of misunderstanding, lack of consideration and of incomplete knowledge among folks who all really want the best for the Grandkids.

The mere fact that you are reading a book titled Caring Grandparents tells me that, for you, it is not that you don't have the best of intentions, but it may be that you need a bit more information about what is and is not working with extended families in today's climate. I probably could have named this chapter "When good intentions aren't enough."

Perhaps a story will illustrate the nuanced difference between intention and best practice a bit better.

A couple who has been friends of mine for a very long time shared this story about when their daughter was about to have her first child. As the time approached, they became excited about becoming New Grandparents. But first let's back up about 9 months. The soon to be Grandmother, Brenda, had been pretty close with her daughter so she held back her opinion when her daughter, Britney, came home and announced that she was going to marry one of her classmates shortly after High School Graduation. They didn't know much about this young man, Car Jr. Actually, they secretly hoped this enthusiasm and romance would pass with time. That hope faded when Brittney soon announced that she was with child. Brenda and her husband Brad prayed about it and decided to make the best of this inauspicious situation by supporting Britany and soon-to-be son-in-law Carl (nicknamed Junior), plans to marry. Part of their attempt to make the best of it was to invite Junior's parents to dinner and get to know them.

The dinner with Carl Sr. and Sarah went well. Ahead of time all agreed that this would be a light and fun gathering devoid of all the questions of what, why and who, this was just a get to know each other dinner. It went well. Carl and Sarah were gregarious and delightful. Britney and Carl Junior were pretty quiet so as not to open Pandora's box at this first meeting. It was decided that they would gather again in the near future. As you may have guessed, everyone got busy planning the near future wedding and as will happen, the what, why and who's didn't come up much. This was a freight train that was in motion so very little attention was placed on the hard questions.

In a few weeks the smallish wedding went off with a minimum of hitches and everyone smiled for the pictures. It had been decided that friends would be asked to give practical gifts for their household. Both families would pitch in, in lieu of wedding gifts they would help the kids get an apartment, some furniture and a few months' rent. Ah, the euphoria of youth and wedded bliss.

The coming months went fairly well. Brittney and Junior each had typical low paying jobs that are available to high school grads, but they squeaked by. The kids actually were pretty responsible for their ages. Of course, transportation was an issue since their used car kept breaking down. Both Britney's dad and Carl Sr. were pretty handy so they kept the kids from being stranded.

Even with their busy lives the Grandparents-to-be interacted enough to communicate about the upcoming birth of their mutual first Grandchild. As the date of this miracle approached it was decided that Britney's Mom and Junior would be in the delivery room and the rest of the family would stand vigil in the waiting room. This is important because sometimes the Paternal Grandmother wants to interject herself into this event and this usually causes tension. Good communication ahead of time, problem averted. The blessed event came off pretty smooth after just two and a half hours of labor. Good Job Britney! Smiles and congratulations abounded that day and, in the days to come.

The celebratory atmosphere was also masking the fact that the kids were already facing mounting financial worries and now Junior was the only breadwinner at his low wage job.

Back at the kids' apartment the practical gifts arrived, and this sleep deprived, insecure young couple began family life in as normal a way as possible. Both Mom's couldn't get enough of their new Grandson Blake. They both pitched in to help Britney and Junior with the baby. Each had their own experiences, so they operated a bit differently when it came to Blake. Britney's Mom was tuned into Britney and would ask her what her wishes were. Mother-in-law Sarah tended to take charge and frequently share her ideas of how things should be done with Britney.

A few days after Blake was born Sarah offered to watch him while Britney got some much-needed rest. Britney woke up to find her newborn son sleeping on his stomach with a blanket covering him and a stuffed animal that Grandma Sarah had bought in the crib with him. Britney, trying to be gracious and grateful for the respite, tried to tell Sarah that her pediatrician and her pre-birth classes had said that the baby is safest on his back with nothing else in the crib. Sarah dismissed this off handedly with a comment that she had raised three healthy kids. This was arrow number one from her mother-in-law.

In less than a week Britney began to show signs of irritability, fatigue and mood swings. Brenda became concerned and began to suspect that Britney's Baby Blues were not subsiding as normal and that this may be Postpartum depression. Brenda had experienced some Postpartum mood swings herself when Britney was born. In the meantime, Sarah was telling Britney that she just needed to get over it and tend to her baby. Britney already felt guilty, exhausted and depressed. As you can imagine this created a lot of tension between these three women. Brenda tried repeatedly to explain the symptoms to Sarah but to no avail. These were arrows numbers 2,3 and 4 from her mother-in-law. In short order Britney and Brenda told Sarah that they didn't need her to babysit. Junior took it personally and he got mad. All this tension did nothing for a new mom suffering through postpartum depression. Needless to say, the effects extended into their future as an extended family. All future attempts to reconcile this kind of attitude were marginal at best.

In the next chapter I will deal with this in more detail, but an attentive and sensitive consideration of the new parents should guide you through the myriads of decisions you will be making on your journey. This is especially true in a heightened emotional situation that includes a young couple and a first Grandchild. Your role should be strictly supportive. It will be helpful to be supportive, but it may be transformative to be affirming and approving of these young parents. Some Grandparents struggle with this concept of remembering that this is their child, not yours. As Grandparents it may be useful to add an 11th commandment, **Thou shalt honor thy Grandchildren's Mother and Father.** It is also useful to have the humility to realize that this is about them and your new Grandchild, not about you. You are entering into a new universe of opportunity that has been created by a thing called "Extended Family". This is an important time to lay a sound foundation of support and consideration with BOTH of the parents. They need enhancers, not critics, especially now.

It is well known that the power of parents and Grandparents operating in unison in the best interest of the Grandchild cannot be overstated. This is Familial Love in action. This synergy adds value to the all-important secure attachment that allows children to grow and thrive. It is not an exaggeration to tout the advantage of a unified effort to offer our little Loves the absolute best chances to develop and grow to their own potential bathed in a sense of feeling Loved.

Over the past 20 years as I have been researching and writing in the Grandparent's Space I have come upon a concise way of thinking about where we find ourselves as Grandparents. It is what I stated in my interview with Jack Canfield and it bears repeating. "Life is complicated, Family life is a multiple of complicated and Extended family life is exponentially complicated."

Please believe me when I say that this is not hyperbole. This is the reality and the challenge of each of us as we consider this quest of becoming the best Grandparent we can become. It requires an assessment of each of the stakeholders in this extended family. It requires a strategy for how we interact in our family and most of all, what it takes to do the best we can for each of our Grandchildren given the circumstances. This WILL require a paradigm shift. I am not at all saying you have to like it, but it is essential to a healthy long term relationship with all of these new family members.

Another of the most overlooked facts of becoming a new Grandparent is that you will do well to recognize the hierarchy of this new extended family. There is a great difference between being the Maternal Grandmother and the Paternal Grandmother. If you stir this in a bowl along with all the swirling emotions, fatigue and stresses of birthing a Grandchild, adding a huge dose of understanding and intentionality will go a long way. Not a judgment of right or wrong, just a fact.

A Caring Grandparent in the 21st Century finds themselves in a very different world than their Grandparents lived in and even less like their Great Grandparents lived in. My maternal Gram would tell us stories of what it was like when they first got water and then electricity in their home. She shared her awe at the advent of TVs, cars, planes, etc. Here we are worrying about AI taking over the world. I tell you this story to set the stage for your success.

Her idea of Grandparenting was that she could bake her way into our hearts, which she did, at huge family gatherings where the family lived locally. They frequently Laughed and Loved around the kitchen table. My Gram held a majestic position of respect, Love and admiration by the entire family. That was back then, today, it may take more than baking skills to go along with that unconditional Love we knew she had for us.

Like it or not in the 21st Century there is a need for us to participate in the process of maintaining civility and peace in our extended families if we hope for the best outcome. Whereby Gram was automatically bestowed her respect and honor it is not so automatic today.

I heard a guest speaker by the name of Ted Page on the Cool Grandpa podcast. Ted is writing a book about what it means to be a "Good Grandpa". To this end he interviewed Tom Browkaw. Tom Browkaw anchored NBC nightly news for 22 years and he also has many other TV shows under his belt. He received the Presidential Medal of Freedom from President Barack Obama plus many other awards. Ted's big question that he asks is, "What is the #1 thing?" The most essential and powerful wisdom you've learned that you want the next generation to know?"

Tom Browkaw's answer was "You have to earn the affection of you children." Wow! That is wisdom for us Caring Grandparents when it comes to our children, their spouses as well as our Grandchildren.

It is understandable that we may have a nostalgia for those bygone times but that is not reality. Wishing and Hoping for those times is not a good strategy, much less a healthy way of approaching the task at hand. Most of us find that our present-day families are somewhat different. Like it or not, our success as a Caring Grandparent lies on the other side of that wall of nostalgia. My hope is that the stories and information in this book will help you understand how to scale that wall and learn what is working and not working in today's family structures and circumstances.

It is not within the scope of this book to get into any of the whys and wherefores, however there are hints in all of these stories. It is my goal to share them as a guide to what is working and what is not working well in today's world. In the past dozen years, I have witnessed some shifts in how Grandparents are adjusting to the times. You may have heard the famous Confucious quote "To know what you know and what you do not know, that is true knowledge". If only it were that simple? My first three books about Grandparenting are riddled with extremely sad stories of folks thinking they knew what was right and feeling the need to try to impose those ideas on family members.

Let me be crystal clear, each of us has the right to be right. Each of us has the right to feel we are right. It is in the act and method of imposing that feeling on others that so many resentments and family tragedies are born. One of the tools I offer to Grandparents the world over is worth repeating. It is the question "How much do you want to pay to be right?" Chapter 6, Restrictions and Alienation will illustrate how some of these sad tails play out. I am intentionally blunt here to be of best service to all Grandparents on behalf of all Grandchildren. To that end I will be sharing stories that are glorious and some that will pull hard at your heart. Please keep these lines of well researched wisdom in mind when you read these tales. Many of these tales illustrate bridges that, once crossed, are very hard to get back over.

I titled this first chapter Our Role with the intention of helping you all to realize that there is, hopefully, a passing of the mantle the moment your first Grandchild cries out. This glorious and joyous moment comes with the changing of the guard. You are off the hook, you are no longer in charge, it is the parents turn to take the helm. You did all you could to raise them for just this moment, just this task. As a Grandparent you are now nominated for best supporting actor. I hope you earn an Oscar for your role in the years to come. Instead of supporting actors I like the term Enhancers. You become the Enhancer in chief.

To the degree you understand this concept you will reap long lasting benefits in the lives of your Grandchildren.

Please go back and read that sentence again!

In our Grandparents community we are fortunate to have a couple that spent many years contributing enormously in the parenting space but now with 40 some Grandchildren have turned their energy and knowledge to contributing to Grandparents all over the world. They are Richard and Linda Eyers. They are renowned teachers, speakers and authors of many books. They tell the story of when they decided to write a book on Grandparenting. They had written many books and presented many programs from the stage together about parenting but shortly after that decision to write a book of Grandparenting it became obvious that it would be better if they wrote two separate books. Richard about Grandfathers "BEING A PROACTIVE GRANDFATHER" and Linda about Grandmothers "GRANDMOTHERING." Our Roles as Grandfathers are markedly different from their roles as Grandmothers. Blessed are the Grandkids that have one of each in their lives.

Two other proactive Grandparents that illustrate the differing roles of Grandpa and Grandma are Grep Payne and Dee Dee Moore.

Greg is not only a Grandpa, several years ago he started the weekly podcast titled "Cool Grandpa". You can find his excellent podcast episodes on his web site at Cool-grandpa.com. He provides a variety of interesting guests that span a wide variety of subjects that pertain to Grandfathers. I have been fortunate enough to participate in a couple of these podcasts. One innovative and valuable podcast is titled "The First Grandfather Cracker Barrel." The value comes from a well-conceived idea that Greg acted on. He describes it best.

The podcast is a round table or cracker barrel discussion for The Cool Grandpa Podcast. The term cracker barrel comes from when, primarily, men would gather in a country store and eat saltine crackers out of a wooden barrel while talking about the weather, news, gossip, etc. I thought this description fits rather well to get a great group of guys together to talk about Grandpa stuff. In this episode, we have the following guests, who comprise our august body: **Frank Pomata**, who joins us from Long Island. **James Lott Jr**. represents Los Angeles (and Brooklyn). **Neil Taft** is from Leland, North Carolina, and **Winn Egan** joins us from Salt Lake City.

Each of these men joins us with various levels of experience and expertise in being a grandfather and promoting the importance of grandfathers in the lives of our grandchildren and communities. This exercise is an enjoyable way to share insights, question our roles, and, most importantly, be able to suggest to each other how we can all be more loving and supportive of the grandchildren in our lives.

During our discussion, we discuss the following subjects:

- **"What do grandchildren want and need?"** – Winn Egan
- **"What have you learned from your grandchildren?"** – Frank Pomata

- "Creating lasting, meaningful connections" – Neil Taft
- "Watching your kids…parent! How do you handle their style vs your style?" – James Lott Jr

You will enjoy our fun and almost instant connection as we focus on how grandfathers can support our grandchildren, our adult children, and their spouses. I have included links below for the episodes each of these men has appeared in as one-on-one guests and how you can connect with James, Frank, Neil, and Winn.

Please share this conversation with friends and family who will enjoy hearing about these subjects and these gentlemen's wisdom.

It was a fun experience for each of us and the information that resulted in this Cracker Barrel is unique and valuable. It is gratifying to me that folks with the same purpose when it comes to Grandchildren can bond over that shared purpose. Not only was it enjoyable but I learned a lot from the other guys. It is heartening to hear these gentlemen put voice to what I know in my heart about Grandfathers. These are truly Caring Grandfathers. My hat is off to Cool Grandpa, Greg for doing this.

Grandfathers tend to take a backseat when it comes to the voices of Grandparenting. What Greg is doing is offering a glimpse of what Grandfathers all over this country do every day to enhance the lives of their Grandchildren and by extension their entire families. Another contribution of Greg's is a very well-presented children's book called "MY GRANDPA'S GRANDPA." I enjoyed it so much that I repackaged it and sent it to my Grandson to read to his Grandson. Great read.

Greg is also a frequent contributor to Grandparents Academy in many ways. He actually has a Master Class in the Academy titled "INTENTIONAL GRANDFATHERING." I have enjoyed and learned from him in this Master Class. You will also find Greg on other podcasts in the Grandparenting space. Suffice it to say that Greg, a Good Grandfather himself, is the go-to guy for all things Grandfathering.

Another valuable resource for Grandparents is Dee Dee Moore. Dee Dee is one of the most knowledgeable Grandmas I know. She is the founder of More than Grand (Morethangrand.com) which is a website with a wealth of knowledge about Grandparenting. More than Grand is the product of Dee Dee's extensive research and considerable expertise coupled with her experience of raising her own children and extrapolating that experience and applying it to being an effective Grandparent. In her own words.

More Than Grand® is full of honest advice and valuable ideas for strengthening the bonds with your grandchildren—and with their parents. Our signature guide for new grandparents, New Grandparent Essentials, gives you all the information you need to realize a supportive partnership and make joyful memories for years to come. Over on the blog, we touch on topics from ways to support expectant parents to how to write letters that foster connection.

I started More Than Grand® when I found out I was going to be a grandmother, I searched the internet for advice on establishing a strong relationship with my grandchildren. Though I found a few articles here and there, most of the grandparenting websites I found seemed to be focused on how much *fun* it is to be a grandparent. I wanted more than craft ideas and sentimental memes, and I suspect you do, too.

I created More Than Grand® with a focus on how *important* it is to be a grandparent. There's plenty of fun along the way, but it's fun with a purpose: to make a positive impact on your grandchild's life.

When Dee Dee first became a Grandmother, she went to the internet for advice. She found the advice lacking and incomplete, so she did her research, and we are blessed with her effort. Her information puts meat on the bones of what it means to be a good Grandparent. I have always counseled my Youth Group kids, my kids and my Grandkids to be the light. Well Dee Dee went looking for some light and didn't find it, so she became the Light.

Her website is an especially good source for New Grandparents. She has also been a guest on Greg Payne's Cool Grandpa podcasts and contributes regularly to Grandparents Academy. Dee Dee is a good source for all things Grandparenting but is exceptional when it comes to New Grandparenting.

I am not asking you to take my word for this. All you need do is to keep on reading. My first three books are full of stories of well-meaning but misguided Grandparents that haven't stopped long enough to consider what it takes to navigate the waters of presumption long enough to take into account the dynamics of family, extended family and relationships in general. Family dynamics, much less extended family dynamics, are tricky at best. My research of Grandparenting informs me that there is a tendency to think that there is an equal hierarchy to the extended family rather than paying attention to those individual members and what they bring to the family. I will submit to you that if you are willing to pause and lean on your wisdom you can be instrumental in making the best of the circumstances and personalities that are now part of your family. Let me repeat a sentence from the previous paragraph. To the degree you understand this concept you will reap long lasting benefits in the lives of your Grandchildren.

Chapter 2

EARLY ON

"We choose our joys and fears long before we experience them."

- Khalil Gibran

Becoming a Caring Grandparent begins considerably BEFORE your first Grandchild is born. You will have plenty of time to form a Lasting Meaningful Connection with this new miracle that is coming into your life "IF". The reason for the capitalization of the word BEFORE is based on many stories and the teaching of the experts in the area of Grandparenting. It actually has a lot to do with our relationships with our own children. It then graduates to our relationship with the partner our child chooses to spend his/her life with. I would suggest that the way we treat this new partner from the outset is predictive of our future as an extended family. If that time has passed it is never too late to start building a healthy relationship. If for no other reason than your future with your Grandchildren. If the past has not played out the way you had hoped, then today is a great day to choose to improve that relationship. I lay all this out to emphasize how very important these spouses are to drawing a direct line connecting our relationships with our Grandchildren. Simply put, the Grandchildren's mother and father are the gatekeepers to your time with your Grandchildren.

In most cases this time of early Grandparenthood goes pretty smoothly. Most of what you will read in this book is intended to help well intentioned Grandparents be aware of how things can be perceived totally differently than they are intended. This is a time of great Joy and celebration, but it is also a time of heightened emotions with a group of people that are just now getting to know each other. I am a firm believer in the goodness of folks, especially Grandparents, given the right information. I am not naive enough to think that there are no bad actors but my interaction with thousands of Grandparents informs me that it is mostly misperceptions and lack of knowledge that causes complications in extended families. It is in this spirit that I have written this and several other books on Grandparenting. My single focus is to raise and maintain the best interest of the Grandchildren.

To this end it will be reasonable for you to re-read that quote by Kahlil Gibran and wonder where this conversation about becoming a New Grandparent is going. I chose that quote because all of my research leads to this time in the life of your family as, possibly, the weakest link in the chain of gaining and maintaining durable, long-term relationships with both parents and the rest of your extended family of your new Grandchild. In effect this is about avoiding avoidable pain.

It is not my intention to be a Debbie Downer, remember my promise of not telling you what you want to hear but rather what is most effective. It is my intent to help new Grandparents to think this process through **before** they have crossed those bridges that are hard to go back over. This is the time in an extended family's experience that new people are introduced. There are two important considerations at this juncture. One is that the newest members of this extended family are not normally people you know very well or have chosen. The second, and by far the most important factor, is that these folks, especially your in-laws, are often the gatekeepers of your access to your Grandchildren. WOW!

I will be willing to bet that those two thoughts were not top of mind as you prepare to welcome a new Love into your life. I encourage you to re-read the story of the mother-in-law in the first chapter. While this is an extreme example of things going very wrong there are literally millions of Grandparents that are experiencing difficulty regularly seeing their Grandkids for reasons connected to this time in the extended family's evolution.

I am not naive enough to suggest that investing this amount of consideration into the time around this New Grandparent event will solve the problems of being cut off from your Grandchildren down the line. Some of the circumstances are so severe and deep rooted that it will require a virtual miracle to keep peace in some extended families. What I do suggest is that "poking the bear", intentionally or not, may initiate unnecessary trouble in paradise. This is a particularly sensitive period of time in the family, and I am advocating that we do all we can to avoid any potential trouble by being as vigilant and considerate as possible.

In my previous book "Good to Great Grandparenting" I told a story of a clueless in-law couple approaching the birth of their first Grandchild. The story is worth repeating here since it points to the essence of a lack of consideration for ALL the players in this drama of what can be a miraculous and life enhancing event in any family. This is an example of well-meaning people who fail to think through and consider their words and actions.

Let's listen in on an all-too-common story surrounding two sets of Grandparents approaching the birth of their first miracle. The maternal

Grandparents Bill and Louise live locally, and they've had a really close relationship with their, now 19-year-old, daughter Lucy. The year before, when their daughter came home to announce that she and Andy were engaged after a short and sometimes tumultuous courtship, they feigned excitement and approval. In the privacy of their own home, however, they often wondered out loud to each other if and just how this whole thing would work out. But they remained quiet about it. Their daughter was determined, so to support her they went along.

Their fun-loving future son in-laws' parents Brad and Mindy were nice enough but the kind of people who would whisk into town for a quick visit with the newly married kids and a dinner with their daughter in-laws' parents and off they would go. At this first dinner the talk was jovial but didn't land as meaningful and sincere, however, once again Bill and Louise, behind closed doors, were concerned.

As the birth event approached Andy's parents again whisked into town to stay at their son's home without checking ahead to see if that was okay. Andy merely announced to Lucy that they were coming to stay with them for a couple of days. He made this announcement to Lucy as they were on the way to the hospital for the delivery. Lucy had too much going on to challenge this, but she did feel uneasy and left out of the conversation.

Everyone rushed to the hospital only to endure a long and difficult labor of nearly 12 hours. Louise was glued to her daughter's bedside with concern and sympathy while Lucy's father was pacing the floor in the waiting room with equal concern. Meanwhile Brad and Mindy were in and out and obviously annoyed that this was taking so long. As the birth approached soon-to-be Grandma Mindy inserted herself into the conversation to say she wanted to be in the delivery room as well. She stated as her reason that this was her first Grandchild too. This time Lucy told her mother that she didn't want anyone but her mother and her husband in the delivery room. You could feel the tension building, as seeds of resentment were being planted.

Now Louise, Lucy's gentle Mom, was being tasked with telling Mindy that her daughter didn't want anyone but her own mother and her husband Andy in the delivery room. This added to the drama of a concerned mother and a now indignant mother in-law at an event steeped in fatigue and emotion. This is a critical juncture in everyone's life. Clueless, father in-law Brad just wants to know what the big deal is.

It is, unfortunately, stories like this that can suck the miracle part right out of the miracle of the birth of the first Grandchild. My point is that this is something, no matter the difficulty, that needs to be talked about ahead of time. Mark my words, this is a time in this and everyone's family life that sets the tone for how the family will function, or not, going forward. This is the time that the seeds of resentment are planted, only to grow over time.

The essential thought is to be **considerate.** It will serve you well to carefully consider the parents' wishes as well as their often sleep-deprived state of anxiety and feeling emotionally overwhelmed. It is also important to consider your relationship, especially with the mother of this miracle. It is normal for the new mother to want her own Mom to be close for this event, but after that the picture is not so clear. It serves all to talk about this openly before the event. If you are the Maternal Grandma, you may be a bit closer to the mother than the Paternal Grandma. While everyone wants to rush in, it is important to offer support but lay back a bit until the appropriate time to be invited in. Please consider that your enthusiasm and willingness to be a part of the event may be more about satisfying your own desire to connect with this new bundle of joy, and not so much about the new family. I have yet to meet the Grandchild that chastised their Grandparent for not being present in the delivery room when they came out.

Emotions are high and memories are long lasting. There will be plenty of bonding time to come and enough Love to go around. One last time, I urge you to consider the importance of this monumental family event.

It is stories like these that point out where the seeds of resentment and anger are planted. Only "IF" the mother-in-law had put herself in the shoes of this scared, tired and insecure 19-year-old birth mother I am confident that the outcome would have been so much better for all concerned. This is not the story of a Mother-in-law with bad intentions, it is merely a story of a New Grandparent that didn't take into consideration the feelings of all those involved. Consider replacing your ego in this moment with an understanding of this moment. A miracle is happening, and some people put themselves ahead of the miracle and the scared 19-year-old girl that is giving this event her all. The revealing truth is that this 19-year-old lady is the person who is the primary decision maker when it comes to how much involvement these Grandparents will have with their Grandchildren in the future. To be succinct, treat the new mother like the gatekeeper for your Grandchild....... because she is.

This seems like a good time to interject one piece of advice to Grandparents that will color ALL your interactions with this new family unit. The time has come to pass the mantle. The time has come to hand over the reins of this family to its proper owners, the parents. They are having THEIR baby and if you play your cards right you will be invited to participate in your Grandchild's life going forward. I hate to be blunt, but this is important enough for me not to sugar coat it. It will serve you well to consider what I just said.

I have a couple of friends that advocate the approach of "Ask, Ask, Ask! This approach does several things, first and foremost it conveys respect and allows the new parents to grow into their rightful positions. This approach also indicates interest in good outcomes, and it cements your position as an Enhancer. My publisher and friend Steve Harrison goes a bit further, he says you should become an Ask Kisser!

Enough preaching. I just want to drive home the point that there are many ways to run at these new relationships in this new extended family. It is in your control and best interest to consider each step, especially early in the process of developing good relations with all of the stakeholders of this expanding family. Plant your flag as a Caring and thoughtful Grandparent.

Another consideration is that, like it or not, there is an often unspoken. hierarchy to an extended family. This is most pronounced as we approach the birth of our Grandchildren. Let me modify that a bit further and call it a Matriarchal structure with the mother of our new miracle seated firmly on the throne. Next in line is the father. Then comes the maternal Grandparents and finally the Paternal Grandparents. Being mindful of this hierarchy will prevent problems as in the previous story. Please also keep in mind that shooting the messenger is still a crime.

Sermon over on the time leading up to our blessed event. Now we can transition to our new life as Superheroes full of Hopes and Dreams and all fired up on the euphoria of this miracle. Now it is time to go out and buy every available toy and fill the baby's room to the point that we can't even walk into that room. NOT! Let's stop and take a look at that for a moment. What is this new creation going to be doing in the coming months? Sleeping (hopefully), eating, pooping, peeing, and crying a lot. When do you suppose this child will have time to play with all these toys? Maybe this is a time to back up and reconsider. Maybe it is time for some Ask Kissing.

Several of the experts in this area of New Grandparents suggest that it will serve the new parents best if we concentrate on what we can do to support and affirm the new parents. Being specific in our asking about what we can do helps. Rather than the normal "Let me know if there is anything I can do" approach it may be better to be specific and ask "Can I fix you and your husband dinner a couple of evenings each week?" or "Give me a list and I will pick up some groceries so you don't have to bundle up the baby and go out in this weather" or even better, "Would you like me to come for a couple hours each afternoon and keep an eye on the baby while you get some much needed rest?"

This is called Enhancing your role as Enhancer. This is the kind of support that adds value to everyone involved.

I realize that there are considerations for proximity and time constraints due to work, etc. This is where that imagination piece comes in handy. I am just suggesting that you support and affirm the new parents in any way that you can. Their job is enormous, and they are doing it without any training. Support is crucial and considerate support will be appreciated especially if it is wrapped in affirmation of them being wonderful parents. The payoff is long term, and it manifests itself in greater appreciation by the new parents and more time with your brand-new Grandchild.

While I am on the subject of Early On, I would like to go back to the idea of this new family hierarchy and address the silent members of this new extended family, the Grandfathers.

When my bride of 30 years and I lived in Charlotte North Carolina I made the mistake of buying a house that was pretty near the Southpark Mall. It is germane to this story that I admit that I married a shopper extraordinaire. Occasionally on a Saturday she would ask me to take her to the mall. I first checked to see if I could find a dentist that would perform an emergency root canal on a Saturday. Failing that I said, Yes Dear I would love to take you shopping. Much of our adventure would put me standing just outside the dressing room in the ladies' section while she tried on a lot of clothes. You know the ole "Does this dress look good? routine. Well, between the occasional "Yes Dear", since there was no place to sit, I was left standing around in the ladies' section trying not to look **anywhere**. Also trying not to look even more conspicuous than I already was, which was impossible. My point is that I didn't feel like I was necessary to this process.

I tell that story to say that I felt much the same way at the hospital when my Grandchildren were born. Grandfathers pretty much get relegated to taxi service and going for coffee. Fear not, Grandpa, your time will come.

I did have one opportunity to step up to the plate as a New Grandpa and I blew it. This was 20 years ago when my Granddaughter Renee was born. It caught us a bit by surprise since she was born a bit prematurely. Grandma Mimi asked me to drive her to the hospital and I of course said Yes. When we got there Renee had already been delivered and her Mom was back in her room and they brought this new, very little, did I say, very little but beautiful baby girl to her Mom. Quite a few of the family were already there. I just stood back by the door while Grandma went in and Oohed and Awed and held the baby. She asked me if I wanted to hold Renee. I panicked and said No. My wife wanted to hand me this 3 ½ pound tiny person and I was afraid I would break her. I am the guy who worked on Jet aircraft, pitted race cars at Daytona Speedway, bungee jumped from 100', spoke to large audiences in arenas and I panicked at this 3 ½ pound miracle. Renee is now this 20-year-old beauty, and she forgives me. Maybe this is why they don't let us Grandpas near the process of this having baby's stuff. Maybe for Grandfathers it should be Later On instead of Early On.

I hasten to add that Grandpas can and do play a significant role in the growth of their Grandchildren. We are endowed with a unique opportunity to add so much value to our Grandchildren. As with the story that began this book you never know what impressions and influence you leave with these young minds. Grandpas add a special kind of icing to this Grandparenting cake.

Chapter 3

THE EXTENDED FAMILY

"A family is a place where principles are hammered and honed on the anvil of everyday living."

- Charles R. Swindoll

If we do our job as parents correctly our kids will leave home and find a life partner. Hopefully that will result in Grandchildren. No matter, the family expands in a way that we don't have much say about. Not only our children's partners but by extension their family members become our extended family. This can be anywhere from exciting to terrifying depending on our children's choices of life partners.

Many plays and movies have been made about family members that go outside of their cultures, races, nationality and/or religions to choose a life partner. Usually, the drama of these plays and movies is based around the unknown and the fears that are fomented. The normal dynamic tension is between tradition and Love. Good luck tradition. Many years ago, I was blessed to get to see the great actor, Jan Pierce in "Fiddler on the Roof" live on Broadway. The song that ran throughout this musical was "Tradition!" The overarching idea that I came away with was "but then on the other hand"! In the end the Patriarch of the family was forced to choose another way to look at his entire life or lose the love of his daughter. Again, good luck Tradition.

It is fair for you to ask where this author is going with this drivel. It is clear to me that almost every family I know deals with a version of this concept. We do not play a major part in the selection process of our children's choices of life partners. I can't recall being asked but when we meet said partner the question becomes, "Now what?" Or as one of my favorite TV dad says at the dinner table of the TV series "Blue Bloods", **It is what you do next that counts.**

In my Youth Ministry days, I was called upon to act wisely about things that could not be changed after the fact. I would sit and listen to the various woes of the various young people in my group. Whether it was an individual or the entire group I relied on a saying that an artist friend of mine made into a plaque that still, 50 years later, hangs in my living room. The saying goes like this. "So sad, Too bad, So what, Now what?"

The wisdom of that saying is that it first recognizes the negative situation, acknowledges the gravity of the situation, states the obvious fact that changing the past is a non-starter and finally asks the question that points to the only course of action. This isn't necessarily the case in all extended families but consideration and care in thinking this through will go a long way to what happens in the future.

Let me restate, wishing it weren't so is not a useful strategy.

This applies doubly if you are the Paternal Grandparents in this extended family. This is just the nature of extended families and the hierarchy of these extended families. I am not asking you to like it. I am just telling you that the research is clear, it is incumbent upon you as Grandparents to find a way to operate within the structure of your extended family if you desire to maintain Lasting Meaningful Connections with your Grandchildren. There is simply no upside for you or your Grandkids to wish things were different. There is, however, a bright upside if you learn what is working and do all that you can to make those kinds of things happen. Lest you think I am advocating that the entire extended family regularly gathers around the campfire, arm in arm, singing Kumbaya, I am not. What I am suggesting is that you at least reserve judgment and at best find common ground. An effective way to frame this idea is to consider that another word for common ground is Grandchildren.

Even though most extended families are pretty functional it is still good to keep your ear to the ground and constantly adjust to the current circumstances. A good example is what happened to me a little over ten years ago.

Almost 20 years ago my son married a delightful young lady, and they brought me this absolutely beautiful and wonderful Granddaughter. Still the Love of my life. However, I digress. When my Granddaughter was around 8 or 9 her parents ran on rocky marital times. They ultimately divorced. During this time my natural tendency would have been to choose to side with my son and the normal outcome of that would have been to alienate my daughter-in-law and consequently resulting in my being cut off from my Granddaughter. By divine wisdom, for which I am eternally grateful, I chose to stay clear of the fray. I continued to respect my daughter-in-law and support how she was raising my Granddaughter. I maintained an open and functional relationship with her when it came to my time with my Granddaughter. To this day she and I have a good relationship and as a result

I enjoy significant and quality time with my still beautiful and wonderful Granddaughter.

I had a wise teacher that once said, "The main thing is to keep the main thing, the main thing." Mission accomplished.

In present day society you have about a 50% chance of being caught in this divorce scenario with one or more of your children. This should be something you look out for and have a strategy in mind for that possibility. It does not mean automatic alienation but that can and does happen in too many cases. This becomes particularly tragic in cases where the Grandparents are an integral part of the raising of their Grandchildren until a fissure happens in the family and their access is completely cut off or severely restricted. Facebook is full of groups with heart wrenching stories about alienated Grandparents. The stories are sad and the solutions, after the fact, are hard, as well as few and far between. What I advocate is that we find a way to preemptively construct our extended families in such a way that we can weather almost any event. I will not be accused of saying that it is easy in any way, but it is possible, and I will say, unequivocally, that our Grandchildren are worth the effort.

When it comes to non-functioning extended families this is usually the way this plays out.

Sam and Barb were sweethearts all through school. They were even the Senior King and Queen at their Philadelphia High School. They graduate and go off to different colleges. They manage to keep the flame alive though and plan to get married right after they both graduate from college. During their 3rd year they reunite at home for Christmas break. They are very much in Love, and they enjoy a nice Christmas together. They plan to go on Spring break together to the panhandle of Florida with many of their classmates. I am old but I think the term is P-A-R-T-Y!

Well, party they did. Shortly after returning to their respective campuses Sam gets a call one evening from Barb. The tears are flowing but when he calms her down, she lets him know that they are pregnant. That next weekend Sam travels to Barb's school. After much discussion and a call home to her parents, Jim and Jenna, it is decided that she will finish the year and move back home to have her baby. Barb and Sam will marry early in June and live with her parents for the summer before Sam returns to finish his last year of school. His parents, Skip and Glenda, while not happy, are okay with the plan. They marry and begin their lives together. They both work and save money over the summer. Sam returns to school and Barb continues to work until the doctor puts her on bedrest late in the fall. Sam, concerned, offers to drop out and come home to be with Barb. Sam's parents interject that under no circumstances should he quit before graduation. Reluctantly he agrees to return to school. Barb doesn't press the issue. He travels home every chance he gets. He stays an extra day now and then and extends his Christmas break to be there for the birth of his daughter, Jackie. She is a beauty, and the family is ecstatic. However, all these absences begin to reflect on his grades, and this infuriates his parents, especially his Dad. He feels pressured but stays the course. Upon graduation he heads back home to be with Barb. Barb is now working and her Mom and Sam's Mom Glenda help out with daycare. Unfortunately, partially due to his grades in college, he has no job offers back home so he takes a job outside of his Finance major which doesn't pay as well. Between the two of them they do manage to get a place to live and make enough to support their new family.

Sam's dad Skip continues to pressure him to begin his career. Sam shares this pressure with Barb which begins to build some tension between her and her father-in-law. While all this is going on Glenda has some health issues and Barb's Mom, Jenna, becomes the main caregiver for baby Jackie. One month leads to the next and suddenly Jackie is two years old. All this time Skip hasn't let up on Sam who begins to drink a little more. To add to the pressures Barb gets pregnant again. This is not an event that is greatly celebrated, especially by Sam's dad. He is overheard by Barb saying to Sam that he is being held back by that woman. This deeply wounds Barb, and she begins to share her feelings with Sam.

This is a defining moment, and, probably out of anger and spite, Sam sends out feelers to see about getting a job in his chosen field. Soon a job comes available in Atlanta Georgia. Secretly they are both glad to take Jackie and get out of town and out from under the hammer of Skip and his constant pressure on Sam. Jenna says she is a bit relieved to get back to her job. The kids pack up and move to Atlanta. Barb is a bit apprehensive since her Mom won't be close by to help, but she supports Sam and his decision to take the first job that comes along. His drinking has been getting worse and she hopes for a new start in a new city to turn things around. As they settle in Sam gets used to the new firm. The pressure his dad hounded him with is replaced by the pressure of the new job. Finance is by nature a demanding field. Produce, produce and produce some more is the mantra. Sam gives it his all but under the weight of quotas he now adds a few drinks at lunch. Barb is once again confined to bed rest so there is also pressure at home when he is not at work. A couple of months later Barb delivers Jackie's brother Ben. All four Grandparents show up for the event. There is a considerable amount of tension, but they manage to get through it. Skip even managed to zip his lip for the most part. After a few days everyone but Barb's mom returned to Philly. Jenna stayed a few weeks to help Barb with the baby. One evening Sam overheard Jenna talking with her husband, Jim, about Sam's drinking.

He didn't tell her he heard this, but he became upset and defensive with Barb knowing she had confided with her Mom about this.

With all the Grandparents back in Philly life went on and Barb went back to work after a couple of months. Things seemed to level off a bit. A few months later Grandpa Skip and Grandma Glenda wanted to come for a visit. The kids, wanting their Grandparents to interact with their Grandkids, said yes. It was a long week for Barb who felt very judged and tense the whole time. One night Skip took Sam out drinking and they both came home very drunk. They woke the babies, and it seemed as if all hell broke loose. Everyone was upset and no one got much sleep.

Barb noticed that not even Glenda was very apologetic. As it turns out she had been dealing with this kind of stuff from her husband for many years. They survived the week. About two months later Barb's mom and dad came for a visit and the contrast was stark. Peace seemed to prevail, and the little ones were showered with love and affection. Jim did notice that Sam always had a drink in his hand. Barb emerged from that week refreshed and feeling optimistic after being bathed in the Loving support of her parents.

This was short-lived because right after they left Sam came home very late and he was really hammered. This time he was loud and abusive toward Barb who was just trying to keep him from waking the babies. From that point on things went downhill for the next year. Jackie, now almost 4, began to ask questions about her daddy's behavior toward her mom. Finally, Barb had enough and confronted Sam about both the drinking and the abuse as well as the fact that even his 4-year-old daughter was noticing. Sam's response was to storm out the door and not come home for two days. You guessed it, he came home drunk and aggressive. Barb tried to quiet him but this time he hit her. She called the police, and they hauled him off to jail. She called her mom who came right away. He got out the next day, but Barb wouldn't let him back in the home. He stayed at a hotel for a couple of days and that weekend he came pounding on the door late one night and demanding entry. It scared Barb, Jenna and the babies. They called the police and this time she filed a restraining order. Things only got worse from here and eventually Barb packed up the kids and her and her mom returned to Philly.

Shortly after they arrived here comes Sam's dad Skip, half drunk, pounding on Jim and Jenna's door just as Sam had done to Barb in Atlanta. He was demanding to see his Grandkids. Jim tried to reason with him but Skip threw a punch. Now the Philly police were called.

To put this long, sad story to bed, Barb filed for divorce, got full custody and remarried a year later to a wonderful man, Jake. In that time, because of his violent past Sam only got periodic supervised visits with his kids. He slowly lost interest and quit traveling back to Philly to see his kids. Within another year Jake adopted Barb's kids. Jackie and Ben are now all grown up with kids of their own. They are both happy, healthy and well adjusted.

To fill in the blanks a bit. Sam's parents tried to get visitation rights through the courts. They spent a lot of money, and it took so long that Jake had legally adopted Jackie and Ben, so the Paternal Grandparents no longer had standing in their case and it was dismissed.

That long story illustrates what happens all too often. The strange twist is that Barb said that if it wasn't for Skip's overheard comment and his drunken violent encounter at her door, she would have gladly let him and Glenda visit with their Grandkids. Actions have cumulative consequences. I also add, mothers have the ultimate power when it comes to time with the Grandkids.

This is just one scenario of where things get jumbled in extended families. In many cases these families will find ways to work things out to a reasonable semblance of normal. An important point is that the longer the extended family teeters on the verge of collapse the greater the odds that it will eventually fall over that cliff. It takes a lot of knowledge, patience and consideration to keep things glued together. You will be best served by becoming the bridge builder of the family. This is critical for the Grandchildren. Regardless of their ages it must be tough for them to figure out these dynamics. It is important to all that if there is any possible way to include all the Grandparents in the lives of our Grandkids it is incumbent upon the adults to make this happen. If the Grandparents are willing and the Grandchildren want their company, there is a way to work things out. This returns to my admonition that these kids deserve more Love not less.

The extended family is complicated but that should not be used as an excuse for not availing these kids to that Love which is a priceless asset in their growth and development. I would ask the adults of this extended family to consider that it should not be the responsibility of the children to figure out a way to make this work.

Chapter 4

CONNECTION TO YOUR GRANDCHILDREN

"Most people just want to know that they Matter, especially our Grandchildren."

- Neil Taft

This is where the rubber hits the road when it comes to being a Caring Grandparent. If you have read this far into this book you probably know that creating a **"Lasting Meaningful Connection"** with each Grandchild is the Holy Grail of Grandparenting. It is you operating at your highest and best self. There are so many elements that go into creating this connection. If you are willing to add knowledge, patience and consideration to your existing intention your outcomes will be greatly enhanced. This is a calling and as you know callings are not short-term deals. To honor this calling, you may be called on to do things you may not think you are capable of. There may be times of disappointment that stretch your heartstrings tight but just keep in mind that those precious Grandchildren are worth every ounce of effort you invest in this process. The payoff is reciprocal, you will benefit when your Grandchildren benefit. It probably won't be easy, congratulations in advance.

Do you remember when Staples Office Supply had their Easy Button promotion? They sold big red EASY buttons. Well one of those buttons won't get the job done when it comes to our Grandkids. Creating and maintaining a Lasting Meaningful Connection to each Grandchild is a doable but daunting task! A daunting task with a ROI (Return on Investment) that can be stratospheric and oh so rewarding. This is one of those things that is guaranteed to pay big dividends regardless of the circumstances. Yes, I hear all of your, yeah buts, however your efforts, especially when started early and executed consistently will leave an indelible impression on your Grandchild no matter what. Even if, God forbid, the extended family gets a bit crazy, you will have left a positive mark on your Grandchildren that they can keep in their back pocket. In these cases, I always ask folks to remember your favorite teacher, aunt, uncle, or your own Grandparent and the impression they left on you, as well as the value they added to your life.

The good news is that a significant majority of you will not suffer from such dysfunctional families. Diligently using all the principles laid out in this book, you have a much better chance at maintaining a Lasting Meaningful Connection with your Grandkids. The **Lasting** part of this formula however may be the most difficult mainly because it involves others. You know your own heart and you can exert your own influence, but you cannot always influence the actions of others. This sounds like a place for your Superpower. This is the place for that angelic patient, superhuman understanding of others thoughts and actions and divinely inspired empathy for someone you may not like and/or agree with. Depending on the circumstances you may be called on to perform beyond what you believe is possible. This is when your role as enhancer may be necessary for others in this extended family whether they deserve it or not.

I think you will have a much easier time with the **Meaningful** part of this Lasting Meaningful Connection. There is a term that sums up an **ideal** connection: Secure Attachment. This is the high-water mark of this kind of connection and, consequently, it is worthy of all our efforts to achieve such a lofty goal. You are a Caring Grandparent and you have got this part hands down.

One of the hallmark characteristics of Secure Attachment is Trust. In relationships this is a sense that each can count on the other. There are all kinds of benefits to a Grandchild who has someone in their life, other than a parent, that helps them build their confidence in themselves. That helps these young folks to believe in themselves.

As Grandparents we can impart a sense of comfort and reliability in a seemingly chaotic world. A safe place, if you will? This kind of attachment pays benefits in all kinds of areas. It helps with self-worth, emotional intelligence, resilience, decision making, etc. Secure attachment manifests itself in healthy relationships, positive mental health as well as all around better outcomes for our Grandchildren. The benefits are many and long lasting.

Notice that I call Secure Attachment a lofty goal. This **Connection** part of this is that feeling of attachment one gets when they feel comfortable that this is the real thing. This is not some passing feeling but a deep-seated knowledge of being cared for. Lofty just means that it is seldom that we get all the planets to line up perfectly but that should not keep us from striving in that direction. I get glimpses of this kind of relationship with one or some of my Grandkids from time to time. Just enough to keep me on the path to being the best Grandpa I can possibly be. Truly blessed are the Grandparents and Grandchildren who can come close to this goal but equally blessed are those of us who keep trying. It is when I am trying with all my might to make this Secure Attachment happen that I know I am on purpose as a Grandparent. I can promise you that absolutely none of the energy you expend in this quest to add value to each and all of your Grandchildren will be wasted. Not all of our efforts will land perfectly but all will have a positive effect, even if we can't see it at the time. Young people remember those who help them feel like they matter. Young people can read intent from across the room.

There are three primary Best Practices for this connection journey.
- Early
- Often
- Consistent

To go one step further I will venture to offer one more practice, Imagination. It was Albert Einstein who said, "Imagination is everything". It certainly influences your continued success in staying connected with ever-growing and ever-changing Grandkids and their families through the years. Imagination will supercharge your effort. Imagination will raise your odds of success exponentially.

While the stories I am sharing don't particularly mirror your family situation it takes imagination to extrapolate the lessons and help to prevent these less-than-ideal things from happening to your family. Also, later in this chapter you will have a chance to apply this fourth practice when it comes to Long Distance Grandparenting. The world is your pallet.

There is a plethora of mediums to connect and communicate with your Grandkids. Even those of us that fear this, in my case, dreaded internet stuff find that as kids grow this may be the most important form of communication to use. One rule that sprinkles your connections with sincerity is imagination. It allows you to "Meet your Grandchildren where they ARE, not, necessarily, where you wish them to be." You may want to read that again.

A few other significant considerations of meeting them where they are; their age, information about their friends, interests and general feelings about themselves. This information piece is most effective coming from their parents but there are many other supplemental sources that I will touch on later in this chapter. For the sake of this discussion my plan is to base this chapter loosely on arbitrary age grouping, but you will come to know best where your own Grandkids are at any particular time. I simply put out some of what is working for others to give you food for thought.

Let's dive in. The first thing you get is a year to 18 months' vacation from the job ahead. I am really going to Love this job. The first year to year and a half of their lives is a get ready time. Year two, the fun will begin in earnest. Are you ready for this exhilarating roller coaster ride?

Starting early means that when they are very young this is a good time to interject what I call a hook. I describe this as a sound and/or fun thing you do that is memorable and entertains a little one. To the very young I usually approach them with a smooching sound as I take my finger and thumb and zero in to steal their nose. Then I put it back. If that is too much for them, I just gently touch them on the nose. They usually smile and come to expect that ritual each time Grandpa Neil is around. For some reason little kids like weird noises, especially when they are attached to some spectacular repeated action. If they are taken aback about you approaching their nose you may switch it up and grab their little toe, etc. The main thing is that you are consistent and that they respond each time. With some little ones, especially the shy ones, it may be ducking behind something or someone and playing the legendary "Hide and Seek." At age two and up til about 10 or 11 years old I like to perform my, now famous, Upside-Down Hug. This is done by slowly grabbing their arm, drawing them to you and then slowly turning them upside down. Giggles begin. While doing this you ask them in a low voice, "Do you know what I Love about you?" They always ask, "What"? When I turn them upside down, I begin to shake their lunch out of them. I say loudly, "EVERYTHING"!!!!! Message delivered! Trust me, they will never forget it. My first Grandson, now 35 years old, 6 feet tall and 240 pounds still, tongue in cheek, asks me for his upside-down hug each time I see him to this day!

Some Grandparents have special secret handshakes, one such really neat Grandpa, Winn Egan has 22 Grandchildren and 15 special handshakes. I'm impressed. While very effective, this is the kind of thing that sticks with that Grandchild and lets them know they are special and that they matter. Some Grandparents have funny nicknames, warm hugs, fresh baked cookies, etc. It gives the kids something special to look forward to each time you see them. This is a good place for a tip; if you always arrive at their door with a gift, they may come to look forward to the gift more than you. You can be more creative than that. Use your imagination. "Just sayin'"

Approaching age two there are a bunch of experiential things you can offer. My favorite go-to is the ice cream store, but then that is almost like cheating. Physical things like the aquarium, petting zoo, walks on the beach, wrestling on the floor, playground, etc. As they grow you have an opportunity/challenge (remember that imagination practice) to figure out new meaningful experiences to have together. Keep in mind that simple is also good when it comes to activities. Laser focused attention is what they are seeking, not necessarily your engineering skills. I also suggest you come to these activities rested. Keep in mind children's fascination with repetition. Grow and change they will. Sometimes the experiences require more energy or get more expensive but are still meaningful and worth it.

The world is your playground. This is a glorious time in the lives of our Grandkids and if we embrace it, for us also. Having said that, I would like you to consider that there is sometimes a temptation to outdo the last experience or the other Grandparents. As I have mentioned earlier, sometimes the simple things are the things that land closest to the mark of meaningful connections. Later in this chapter I tell a story of my nephews, two potatoes, an orange, a few pots and pans and an empty Coca Cola bottle on the kitchen floor. The most important thing to every child is your laser focused attention on them. They want to feel like they matter and that can be done by walking around the block hand in hand. Don't worry Grandpa, there is always fingernail polish and make up remover. I also understand that finger paint easily washes out of your clothes. You can always enlist the help of your creator and take advantage of a sunrise, sunset or a walk in the rain. Just being totally present is the gift.

One couple I know has 42 Grandchildren. They are really all in when it comes to this Grandparenting stuff. They do a lot of amazing things with and for their Grandkids. One of the remarkable things they do is that when their Grands are around the age of 16, they take a few at a time on a week-long RV trip around the country. A commitment for sure but an unforgettable memory with Grandma and Grandpa in their teen years. Let your imagination be your guide, the sky's the limit.

Speaking of the sky, my now 35-year-old Grandson has cherished and still mentions a time he and I flew over Chimney Rock, North Carolina when he was about 12 years old. Now that is a Lasting Meaningful Connection we will always remember.

My now 20-year-old College Sophomore Granddaughter still talks about those years when just she and I would go for a special pre-dawn stop at the convenience store on our way to the beach each year for her special birthday sunrise on the beach with Grandpa. Laser focused attention during a literally everyday event of a sunrise. There may not be an Easy Button for these experiences but there is a huge payoff for both the Grandchild and the Grandparent. Remember, there can be magic in simplicity.

Sometimes due to distance or other circumstances gift giving is the only avenue to make special connections for special events. In a society of abundance, even with planning and a ton of forethought, gifts don't normally leave such lasting memories as experiences do. It may be precisely because they are easier and more convenient, but it may also be that a gift is usually one among-many-deal. If a gift is the best we can do, the impact will be directly proportional to the imagination and meaning you put into choosing the right thing for a gift that is wrapped in a thoughtful and memorable way. One caveat that the experts offer is that a few thoughtfully given items outperform a room full of STUFF every time. Enough said.

As I alluded to above, I am reminded of when my now grown nephews were about 2 and 4. I went to visit my oldest sister and brother-in-law at their tiny apartment in Rochester NY where he was in grad school at the time. Suffice it to say that their budget was tight. I joined those two boys on the kitchen floor playing with a couple of potatoes, an orange, two pots and an empty Coca Cola bottle. Those now 50 something guys were as happy as pigs in slop on that kitchen floor playing with their uncle. That was a happy time and it taught me a good lesson of just how little it takes to connect with our little Loved ones.

To expand on the idea of gift giving there are considerations that can add so much value to the simplest of gifts. Every gift you give to your Grandchildren will be enhanced if you first have a conversation with their parents. This is a twofer. Not only will you have a better chance of getting a meaningful gift for your Grandchild, but you will also be honoring their parents and considering their wishes as well. Let's look at a scenario that best exemplifies the pitfalls inherent in this idea.

Say your daughter has one son who is 9 years old. They live 10 hours away. You decide to get him a racing board game because you and he share an interest in cars and racing. If you bypass the parental discussion, you may create one or both of two outcomes. If the parents don't have time or knowledge of racing to play with the child, the game may sit idle or even worse you may be imposing on the parents to take their time to learn about and play this game. I am sure you get my point.

An example of having said conversation and the benefits of it can be derived from my very recent conversation with my son and daughter-in-law. My now 15-year-old Grandson says he wants to eventually join the Air Force and fly planes. This speaks loudly to Grandpa's interest in flying as well as my hope and dreams for the future of my Grandson. To gauge his earnestness, I proposed that for his 16th birthday that is coming up I take him flying and get him a virtual reality headset video that he can use on his gaming headset for him to experience flying firsthand. Sounds logical, meaningful and productive. So, I first ran it by Mom and Dad. They approved of the going flying part but, unbeknownst to me he is restricted from video games because of repeated noncompliance with house rules surrounding screen time and study.

Conversation=Crisis averted. We will still do the flying part and I will continue to encourage his interest, but I won't be the Grandparent that finds himself in parental time out.

There is a slew of considerations in addition to the conversation with parents. Some of these include things like; Age, interests, personality, cultural norms, practicality, educational values, etc. Once you have settled on those considerations you can add value to a gift in the way you present it. Even a practical gift can be enhanced with a great wrapping job or a meaningful note.

I just ordered my soon-to-be College Freshman Granddaughter a desk lamp for her dorm room from Amazon. Now I can't add much to the Amazon box wrapping part, but they allow for sending a message with the gift. My note to her is "Since you light up my life!" It is the little things that can sometimes make the most of a gift, albeit a boring and practical gift.

Gift giving can be meaningful or a slippery slope of more and better, competition among Grandparents, burdensome for parents, etc. As in most things Grandparenting, a partnership with the parents surrounding gifts is valuable for all concerned. I mentioned earlier in this chapter that if you show up at their house with a gift in hand every time the Grandkids may look more forward to the gift than to you.

You may ask, "What if they live in another city?' I am glad you ask.. That very question perplexes many Grandparents who are fearful of losing touch with their Grandchildren once they move away.

This is where that thing called the internet comes in handy. If this causes you pause, don't feel like the Lone Ranger, it still makes my stomach twitch. There are, however, three gifts from the universe to long distance Grandparents everywhere. They are called Zoom, Facetime Phone conversations and believe it or not Snail Mail.

Well, let me offer a fourth gift. To guide us through these often-confusing issues there is a magic lady by the name of Dr. Kerry Byrne. Dr. Byrne is a research scientist who has founded and operates a company connected to a web site, [Thelongdistancegrandparent.com]. She is the creative consummate expert in connecting with and staying connected to your long distant Grandkids. Her imagination is fabulous, and it is guaranteed to spur your own imagination. What she presents is empirically based and tested methods that work. Dr. Byrne says her Superpower is taking research evidence and turning it into practical, useful strategies and practices. In Dr. Kerry Byrnes' own words of what her web site is about.

- We see how hard you're trying to wrap your heart around what it is to be a long-distance grandparent, trying to wrap your head around how to make the whole thing work.
- We don't sugar coat it.
- We say how it is.

We know that every grandparent is different and that every family context has its own challenges. We understand that you may need different types of support at different times.

And it's ok. We're here regardless. Here for ALL of it.

Wherever you are in your journey, you can rely on The Long-Distance Grandparent to give you a trusted single source of support that is not only evidence-backed, relatable & adaptable to different circumstances but also sense-checked and peer-tested (so we know it really works).

For those of us that didn't grow up with technology she can guide us all to many great connecting experiences with our young Grandkids. What I found to be unique about her approach is that she finds a way to encompass the new and the old technologies in a very effective way. It doesn't stop there. The beauty of what Kerry has created is that it works just as well with physical visits and local Grandparents spending time with their Grandchildren. The only ingredients you are required to provide is your imagination and your intention of staying connected to your Grandchildren.

One interesting aspect of The Long Distant Grandparent site is that it offers you more than just getting you comfortable with communicating effectively over the internet, it also encompasses a lot of interesting and effective ideas about a lot of meaningful connection techniques and even snail mail. This is a way for us to stand out as Grandparents. Your Grandchildren get to regularly see and interact with you on screen. In addition, who doesn't like getting something in the mail with your name on it. You can participate in the opening over video or Zoom. It is the next best thing to being there. They can make the connection to your smiling face. I told you this Dr. Byrnes is magic. To further enhance this mail idea, Kerry advocates that you send things in an envelope that is customized to that specific child. Things like envelopes being in that child's favorite color with polka dots or smiley faces or having stickers of their favorite Superhero on it. Additionally, the envelope can be lumpy or large. Just imagine the smile you will create on your Grandchild's face when this arrives with their name on the front. Then the smile you will be able to see on the video or Zoom.

I urge you to check out this mind-expanding site, especially if you have young Grandchildren. Thelongdistancegrandparent.com is packed with things like support for Grandparents, Ideas galore and learning materials. My promise is that you will be plussed by this extraordinary lady.

As you know by now, I am all about being proactive in creating these connections with our Grandkids. The reason I think what Dr. Byrne has created is so very important is due partially to the timing in the evolution of the family. Previously I proffered three best practices (early, often and consistent) for your connection journey and then I added a fourth. What Dr. Byrne offers through her work and web site is all four of those elements, but it comes at a time in the family evolution that is critical. Families with young children are most open to connection with Grandparents. I think this is a crucial time to establish and enhance the concept of Secure Attachment with your Grandkids but even more importantly with their parents. The greater your success in doing this at this time in the families of your Grandchildren the greater your chances will be to create those Lasting Meaningful Connections.

Another foundational method of staying connected to our young Grandkids is through reading. My favorite reading program is the creation of one of our national treasures, Dolly Parton. This "Grand Angel" is the founder of a program called Imagination Library, now with over 30 years of service to millions. Imagination Library sends a different age-appropriate book to each child each month with their name on the envelope. This creates an anticipation and joy that instills a love of reading in these kids. It is worth checking out. There are some availability steps but if your Grandchild qualifies this will elevate you to really, really wonderful Grandparent status. You can go to Imaginationlibrary.com for more information.

Dolly states that this is her way of giving back. She was inspired by her father's inability to read or write. The program started as a local effort in Dolly's home, Sevier County, Tennessee.

Additionally, there is also a reading program for very young minds that partners with Pediatricians around the country that offer age-appropriate books on an ongoing basis. This can be checked out at Reachoutandread.org.

There are now almost a half million families enrolled in a program called Freereadingprogram.com

More good news. Due to the magic of technology and those wonderful things called Zoom, Facetime and the internet you can read to and with your Grandchildren no matter how far apart you live. Your grandchild gets to view you in your own voice while you turn the pages. They can see you creating meaningful connections. Ain't life Grand?

Lest I overwhelm you I trust you will recognize that there are many resources that will enhance your connections with your young Grandchildren. Just Google "**reading programs for kids.**"

Before we leave the subject of reading, one of the forces for good in our Grandparenting community that I introduced you to in the first chapter is Greg Payne AKA Cool Grandpa. Greg has written a wonderful children's book called "MY GRANDPA'S GRANDPA." This is a good book for small children. I sent it on to my Grandson to read to my Great Grandson.

Now we enter those preteen years when sustained conversations are a bit more challenging.

I find reading is still a powerful connecting force. I always ask my preteen and teen Grandkids what they are reading these days. It gives me a window into their interests. I have a method of sneaking my nose under their tent of interests in that I find an interest they have, I then research what is out there,

I buy a book I think will connect with them and read it. If I find it interesting and appropriate I will order a copy on Amazon and have it sent to them in their name. I will call them and tell them what I am up to and for them to look out for the delivery. This is where my approach may differ from some others, but I don't ask about it again until they bring it up. So far, this method hasn't failed, it eventually comes up and we have a mutually interesting book and interest to discuss. Home run!

My now 15-year-old Grandson is a delightful young man and we have come a long way in our weekly conversations. He lives about 6 hours away, so my visits are every few months. Between those visits are filled with almost weekly conversations while the Grandkids are on their way to church on Sunday mornings. Yesterday's conversation was about how he used the battery powered Sawzall that I bequeathed to his dad to remove some small tree stumps in their front yard. He was sooooo proud and I beamed to think he wanted to share that pride with his ole Grandpa. I reflect to a time when he was 9 or 10. Let me say that he is not like my chatterbox son, so our conversations went something like this. Good Morning Storm (nickname at the time) how are you? "Fine." What exciting things are going on for you this week? "Nothing."

How is school? (stupidest question on the planet), he answered "OK."

Are you sensing a pattern here? Well, there is Hope for the Flowers. Grandpa Neil stepped up his game and began to ask better questions and with the help of his parents I learned more about his interests. We serendipitously hit on the subject of Gaming and he lit up. True confession, I had to take a crash course in the lingo of gaming, but it worked. My proof came about 4 years later when his big sister Graduated high school in Winston-Salem NC. This is about a 4-hour drive back to where my Grandkids live in the mountains of

Western NC. To my surprise and great pleasure my Grandson asked if he could ride back with me. Just the two of us for 4 hours in the car. It was really a fun and conversation filled ride. As we approached his driveway he said, and I quote, "Grandpa Neil I really like riding with you, we talk about the most interesting things. That is not always the case when I ride in the car with the family." I was over the moon blown away. What a change, he grew up and I learned to ask better questions. There is always Hope. Oh, Happy Day!

My Grandchildren are mostly in their mid to late teens, so this is my area of expertise. I say that tongue in cheek.

Hands down the almost singular mode of communication with teens is Social Media of one form or another. I was recently challenged even further than before to learn a new social media platform. My almost Freshman College Granddaughter is on a student cross-cultural trip sponsored by the State Department to Tajikistan. This is a landlocked country lying in the heart of Central Asia. All I know is that they speak Persian and are surrounded by a bunch of those "Stan" countries as well as China. Besides being immensely proud of my Granddaughter for learning Persian and venturing on this educational trip, I found out I must use WhatsApp to communicate with her over there. Here we go again with yet another app, but she is worth it.

Everything having to do with Social Media is as unique as your relationship with each of your Grandchildren. I for one tell my Grandkids what I am doing every step of the way, and they are open to me being active when it comes to looking out for them on the platforms they are on.

I will let you all in on my secret weapon that you can choose to do or not. My now world-traveling 18-year-old Granddaughter taught me this. I found that

I have a secret weapon when it comes to keeping up with what is going on in the world of my three teen Grandkids and my two teen Great Grandkids. Are you ready for this? It is Social Media. Now before you burn this book let me explain a few things. Where would you go if you wanted to learn about Social Media? You guessed it, your Grandkids. They Love to show off their expertise on some interesting platforms. It is true that these Social Media platforms will allow you as a Grandparent to observe without you even having to join them. Even if you choose to join these platforms you can observe without having to interact on them. Let me repeat that, you get to observe. Let me repeat the repeat of that fact, you get to observe. This is tantamount to being a fly on the wall of what your Grandchildren talk about all day long. Now if this is an unfair advantage that doesn't change the fact that it exists. I don't use this fact to spy on them, as a matter of fact I don't always follow them or join my Grandkids on their profiles. I use this observation opportunity to keep my finger on the pulse of what they are encountering, and this informs my conversations with them. Another approach is to ask your Grandkids for permission to follow them on the various platforms. This is kind of like sitting with them every day in the lunchroom and listening in on conversations with their friends. Please note that I suggest you ask them if you can follow them. Most will say yes. The advantage of observing is that you have a much better chance of asking them high quality questions as well as meeting them where they are. The bonus is that you can look out for things like bullying, etc.

It may be concerning but if you think you can shield them from this stuff....... well, that train has already left the station. I choose to learn what I can about their world so I can discuss it directly with my Grandkids, and if there is sufficient alarm, with their parents.

Some Grandparents do more than follow their Grandkids on these platforms. They may choose to comment, etc. One 87-year-old Grandpa partnered with his Granddaughter, and they created unique content. They have garnered over 2 million followers. I don't do this myself because I think this is their space, nor do I think I am that cool, but I do check in to be sure they aren't being bullied, etc. This is especially true if your Grandchild is having a tough time in school.

The decisions you make around Social Media are individual but I just want to put this out there for you to consider. Your particular relationship with each of your Grandkids will dictate what path you choose when it comes to Social Media.

My three favorite internet tools are Text, Facebook messaging and now WhatsApp. Many younger folks are migrating away from Facebook, but I don't know of any that don't respond to texts. I use text primarily to add maximum value to each of my Grandkids on average once a week. I call them "Electronic Hugs." My favorite text is simple, "Just thought of you and it made me smile". My other favorite is, "You are Supercalifragilisticexpialidocious!" Those are well guaranteed to hit the mark every time. They serve as the electronic version of caffeine. My teen Grandkids Love them and almost always respond quickly with a "Love you too.".

As you can see my venture into Social Media is limited and very transparent to my Grandkids. As Grandparents there is still much to learn, and this is one of those areas of knowledge that didn't even exist until recently. It is also a changing landscape. Like most things that have value it also has some areas that require caution. It will serve you well to pick one or two platforms, ask your Grandchildren to help you with them and then learn about that platform until you have a good understanding of that platform's features. Yes, I understand that this will require you to read the dreaded terms of service agreement or at least some of them, privacy setting, Safely connecting, Account security, etc.

To be sure you understand these platforms sufficiently it will require you to go further than your Grandkids usually go to know what to be cautious about. Some of the primary concerns you should have are about things like; Your account security, Healthy usage, Cybersecurity concerns, your own digital footprint and how this can affect your friends and family. I know this is a lot but this is the only way you can be sure that you don't fall prey to the myriad of scams and phishing attempts that inhabit some of these platforms. You can use them for good and to add value to your relationship to your Grandkids but, as in everything Grandparenting, the more you know the more value you can add. My intent is not to scare you. My efforts on these cautions are two-fold, first to educate you on the possible dangers you and your Grandkids are exposed to and second to help you be smart about your use of Social Media. Some folks are blindly hoping that these platforms will look out for the best interests of their users. Very bad news, these platforms have a fiduciary responsibility to their stockholders, not their users. Please proceed with caution.

Chapter 5

OUR LEGACY

"I've learned that people will forget what you said, people will forget what you did, but people will never forget how you made them feel."

- Maya Angelou

In Grandparenting there is a score card. It comes in the form of the stories they will sit around the Thanksgiving table and tell about us after we are gone. It is the occasional "I remember when Grandpa took us to………. or Grandma always made us…………. It is also the values we have shared and that our Grandchildren live by. Our Legacy transcends what we said or did, it will be who our Grandchildren perceived us to be. Keep in mind that what we do speaks so loudly it is hard for them to hear what we say. I don't know about you, but I am shooting for "Grandpa Neil was a Loving and Lovable guy who always left you with more than you had when he arrived." A lofty goal indeed but it remains my daily prayer.

The other day I was listening to a podcast of Cool Grandpa, AKA Greg Payne. His guest was a young lady who had been on his podcast some 3 years earlier also. Her name is Adrienne Davis. Adrienne is a Health and Wellness coach who, through a combination of plant-based nutrition and nature therapy has created a holistic approach to living a healthy lifestyle that is effective in helping adults and children overcome physical and mental health challenges by eating more plants and spending time outdoors. My interest peaked when she told of how effective this treatment was for Type 2 Diabetes, panic attacks, etc. As she shared her own experiences growing up it reminded me that in many cases less is more. It brings to mind a quote by Walt Whitman; "The art of art, the glory of expression and the sunshine of the light of letters, is simplicity." My experience and the stories of many Grandparents bear this out.

This point was made even more poignant as she told the story of when she lived with her Grandparents through her formative years. The most amazing part of her story is that it wasn't monumental Aha moments that shaped her love of nature, it was more what I call extraordinary-ordinary moments. Things like her Granddad putting the little black trailer behind the lawn tractor and allowing her to ride in it while he cut the grass. A meaningful connection. Things like hiking in the woods, fishing in the pond, special handshakes. More magic moment connections.

When I was a Youth Minister and had the opportunity to teach aspiring youth ministers, I emphasized that the primary qualification for youth ministry is being present. Adrienne's Grandpa had that one figured out and now she is living out that Legacy he left with her.

Her Grandpa could have understandably plopped her in front of the TV while he went and cut the grass. He could have gone out to his shop and piddled instead of going for a hike with her. Instead, he included her, he was present to her and now she is living out what she gained from him and as legacies work out she is now helping others. Even if you don't believe in magic, that is pretty much magic.

It is in the way we live our lives that we are most effective at leaving our Legacy to these young impressionable minds. When my first Grandson was born, I remember sitting in the waiting room daydreaming about being in my living room one day pontificating all of my wisdom to his hungry young ears. Guess what, he now tells me it had more to do with him tagging along with me, doing the everyday things I did while he was growing up. Yes, there are teaching moments, and I am not slighting them but being present, inclusion, extraordinary-ordinary moments are every bit as impressive on young minds as the big moments. If you will recall, it was the fact that I persevered and learned my Grandson's interests that precipitated that meaningful 4-hour ride home from his sister's graduation. It was the fact that my first Grandson and I shared a love for everything mechanical that led to our best times together. Find the interest and SIMPLY mine it for opportunities.

Many Grandparents I have spoken with are concerned about their Grandchildren's Spiritual growth and rightfully so. This is probably the greatest gift you can offer your Grandchildren. Their Spiritual development will probably have the greatest impact on their lives and be the most helpful to them in the future. As Grandparents we are endowed with exceptional powers just because of the position a Caring Grandparent holds in the family. Be careful not to squander this unique opportunity.

Here I would like to approach this part of our Legacy by talking first about Religion and then about Spirituality. I think both are important and I am sharing my opinion of how I have chosen to impart my personal values to my children, Grandchildren, Great Grandchildren and now my Great- Great Grandchild. My experience is just that, it is my experience.

Religion first. Most families I have interviewed have started the religious education of their own children with the faith they brought to the family. In my case it was Catholicism on my Mom's side and Protestantism on my Dad's side. My maternal Grandparents, Gram and Grandpa Roddy, were the most influential in my upbringing. We lived with them after Dad died when I was about 12. Gram was a devout Catholic and my Grandpa was the kind of Gramps that sat on the front porch drinking beer while Mom and Gram walked us kids up the street to attend Mass every Sunday. Grandpa Roddy died when I was young, so I am not sure of his religion. My paternal Grandparents were Protestant but again I have no memory of my Grandpa on that side of the family. Grandpa Taft died before I was born. Now my Grandma on my Dad's side was a strong personality, and I don't ever recall her even mentioning religion. True confession time, my only memories of my Dads Mom were her barking out orders and me being in perpetual trouble with her. That was probably due more to my behavior than who she was.

Mom and Dad married and moved us to Florida when I was 4. Mom being Catholic and Dad being Protestant agreed to raise us kids Catholic. Dad dressed up and went to church with us on Christmas and Easter. Fond memories even though I remember that he looked awfully uncomfortable sitting there in that pew.

I would say that we were pretty religious. My brother and I were both altar boys, my big sister considered becoming a Nun and we all went to Catholic school and had Nuns as teachers. As I grew, I was always pretty active in my church. I even married a young lady who had gone to the novitiate to study to be a Nun. She had taken a few years off for a medical sabbatical and that is when I met her. A couple of years later we married in a palatial cathedral type church. The next year after my son was born, we moved from Cincinnati

Ohio to the old family home in Ft. Lauderdale, Florida.

We joined our small Catholic church just down the street. That is where our second child, my daughter, was christened. My wife and I were in the choir, I was on the parish council, we assisted in overseas mission work, etc. This was repeated for each church thereafter. When the kids were preteens I became the Youth Minister at our church in Asheville, North Carolina. My wife and I decided that our kids would be a part of our work. I couldn't wrap my head around leaving our children with a babysitter to go off and minister to teenagers, so the deal was we came as a family package. Those couple dozen teens embraced this idea. Our kids were part of everything we did in the ensuing 3 ½ years as a Youth Group. Those were glorious years, but I had promised my son when I started that in 3 years when he became a freshman in High School that I would step aside. I felt it important that he had someone besides his dad as a youth pastor. This is an important position in a young person's development, and I wanted him to have a good experience. He appreciated that and now in his 50s he is a Music Minister at a church in Western North Carolina near where he grew up. My daughter and her husband are active and integral to their church here in Coastal North Carolina.

I tell the belabored story to set the stage for the religious Legacy I have left for my own late teen Grandchildren. Each Sunday morning, I get a call from one or all three of them to touch base while they are on their way to church. This is my favorite call each week. I refer to it as Sacred time. Each one of the three are active in their youth groups and various ministries at their church. I am a proud and blessed Grandpa.

While I believe that it is valuable for the parents and Grandparents to model a good foundational religious experience for kids while they are small and growing, I also believe that this is not enough. I think there is a step beyond. The analogy that comes to mind is that after teaching them how to handle this new contraption, the parent now letting go of the bicycle seat as their child learns to ride. My moment can best be illustrated by retelling an experience that I shared in my last book.

When I was at the end of my Youth Ministry days, I had a profound event surrounding the final retreat I was taking my group on. The plan was to go to Hot Springs, North Carolina. This is a beautiful and quaint mountain town in the far reaches of Western North Carolina. It has a hostel sponsored by a small Catholic community. This hostel is a respite for the hikers of the Appalachian Trail where the hikers can shower and rest on their trek along the trail. It is a great place, especially for a retreat. Our group fundraised, planned and joyously anticipated this trip as my family, and I did.

Just the month before our church had been assigned a new pastor. Prior to his arrival I had enjoyed the unconditional support of all the parents and the previous pastors of our community. He was a mature priest with the designation of Monsignor, which in the Catholic Church signified rank. His reputation of being an old school authoritarian administrator preceded him. In our few meetings during that first month, I showed considerable restraint and respect for his position as I described the history of my tenure as Youth Minister. I could tell he was not enthusiastic about how I had ministered to this point but as they say, it was what it was. As a matter of fact our group was a standout in the Diocese when it came to participation in youth groups. Our attendance held at around 25 each week which is astonishing for teenagers at that time. We produced many Diocesan Youth leaders and supported other youth ministries regularly.

On the eve of the departure for our retreat I get a call at home from our new pastor. I told him that all was on track and the priest at the Hostel in Hot Springs was eagerly awaiting our arrival and looked forward to helping with the retreat. Toward the end of the conversation the Monsignor got very serious, and it was then that I realized why he called. He put on his authoritarian voice and said, "Mr. Taft, I want you to make those young people obey the word of God." I paused for a moment before delivering my considered, divinely guided response which was "Monsignor, the best I can do is to help them to want to obey the word of God." Dead silence ensued. After a long moment I said, "Thank You for calling Monsignor."

Just so I don't leave you wondering, we had a deeply meaningful retreat that some of the kids would refer to for years to come. It was early spring, and we had a magical dusting of snow one morning. We found a single emerging Dandelion poking through the light snowfall, so we circled that for morning devotion. I must admit that on that day our morning prayer and reflection kind of turned into a friendly snowball fight. I call that Spiritual Serendipity.

My continuing education back then included reading folks like Margaret Mead. She was an American cultural anthropologist who was a media source mainly in the 1960s and 70s. One of her quotes informed my approach to my teaching. She said, "Children must be taught how to think, not what to think." Another of my teaching guides was a man named Dr. Charles Shedd. He was an American Presbyterian minister and a master communicator of homespun wisdom. In one of his books he wrote, "You don't have to teach teens what is right and wrong, they already know that what is best to teach them at this age is what is smart." I found this to be a wise observation, especially when it came to my teenagers.

I was asked at my final meeting with the parents of my teens what I came away from this teaching experience with. My answer was, "I wasn't sure what to expect back when I apprehensively took on this role but what I found is that these kids taught me, by word and by example, a lot about how to be a Spiritual Loving and Lovable person. For that I will be forever Grateful."

My experience with my now almost grown Grandkids is not any different. I help them to know that they are not apprentice people, they are the real and glorious thing. I honor, appreciate and celebrate who they are and meet them right where they are. All of my Grand, Great and now Great-great Grandkids know they matter to me and to the universe. That is the Legacy I leave with each and all of them.

Chapter 6

RESTRICTIONS AND ALIENATION

"There's nothing written in the Bible, Old or New Testament, that says, 'If you believe in Me, you ain't going to have no troubles."

- Ray Charles

The burning question I get asked most is "How did this happen?" How can well-meaning Grandparents and well-meaning parents get so far apart on this journey of raising our Grandkids? As you can imagine the answer to that question is beyond complicated and it varies in each and every case of complicated extended family relationships. I do have two clues to share. The first is my answer to Jack Canfield about what the most common misperception that Grandparents have

My answer was, "Grandparents often think that Grandparenting will come naturally. Some think it is kind of like falling off a log." That may be true for some very small minority of Grandparents but for the rest of us you should know that learning and intentionality are the key to success with our Grandchildren.

Like life in general, there are no free lunches when it comes to quality connections with our Grandkids. There is, however, a tremendous amount of Joy to be had but it only follows our paying close attention, meeting our Grandchildren where they are and applying our own brand of Intentional Love and Caring."

If you couple that with the findings of a recent poll of parents that states in a recent AARP article. Parents reported their top three most common areas of disagreement with Grandparents about Grandchildren. According to a new poll, they are; are 57 percent said discipline, 44 percent said meals and snacks and 36 percent said screen time. I find this a hopeful place to start both parents and Grandparents on a path to understanding some major points of difference to home in on. It is instructive to realize that the six most significant people in a child's life operating from the best of intentions can be this far apart in these three areas.

Two mainly well-intentioned groups of people with the same desire for the best interests of these children that are that far apart indicates that we have what was succinctly stated in an old movie "What we have here is a failure to communicate." A disconnect that seems to be getting worse as time passes. I stated elsewhere in this book that there are some significant sociological reasons for this disconnect but I for one want to find a path to reversing this trend. I see one path to this reversal being a shift in the paradigm of Parent/Grandparent responsibilities and a ton of education and communication.

I am not discounting how complicated this silent epidemic is; I am merely pointing to one possible starting point. The status quo is not acceptable. There are people of Hope that are working hard to find some way through this devastating dilemma. It is devastating for all. The Grandparents suffer. The parents are withholding Love from their own Grandchildren and their parents, this has to be laden with a ton of guilt and confusion. The

Grandchildren suffer the most. This is worth a lot more effort and a lot less avoidance of what is happening to 10's of millions of extended family members. I will go so far as to label a solution to this crisis as essential. It is to that end that I sit here each morning at 4:30 AM and write this book.

There is some good news, however, the vast majority of families find a way to navigate the multitude of challenges that are part of this thing we call an extended family. For those folks I recommend you, daily, bow your head and meditate on your blessings, and at the same time remain vigilant. Part of staying vigilant is to learn about and offer support to those Grandparents that are suffering such a fate as alienation and restriction. For those Grandparents that experience troubles in their family structure there are ways around and through these challenges, but they are far from easy. It is to each of you that I dedicate this section of the book.

To the point of the vast majority of you that enjoy relative normality in your extended family I invite you to join with like-minded folks every chance you get. Caring Grandparents must stick together, support and share.

Strangely enough, one of the best sources of this stick-togetherness is not actually a Grandparent himself but rather the product of some extraordinary Grandparents. Aaron Larsen has merged his enormous talent, knowledge of social media, expertise in the organization, and creation of good expert information with his experience of his empowering relationship with his Grandparents to produce GrandparentsAcademy.com (a.k.a. "Grandparents Academy"). Grandparents Academy is the most current and significant repository of information about Grandparenting. Here is how Aaron describes it on his website:

Founded on National Grandparents Day in 2011 while living with his Granny Grit, Grandparents Academy was inspired by the life-changing lessons and experiences Aaron Larsen received from his grandparents. After graduating college during the Great Recession, Aaron went to "Grand School", spending four years living with his grandparents in his early 20s. After caring for his Grandpa Grit in his final year of life, Aaron created the world's first online academy for grandparents designed to help them grow meaningful relationships and rich legacies with their loved ones. To date, Grandparents Academy resources have reached millions of grandparents worldwide.

Grandparents Academy serves grandparents of all backgrounds. From long distance grandparents to live in grandparents, grandparents raising their grandchildren and those who are undeservedly estranged or alienated from them. Our amazing students are intentional grandparents who love their grandkids, are lifelong learners and wish to cultivate a lasting legacy. Grandparents Academy is where grandparents go to grow up.

One of Grandparents Academy's signature events is "Grandparents Week" which extends National Grandparents Day into the largest online celebration and educational event for grandparents of its kind. It's free to attend and chock full of insightful presentations, prizes, and other goodies for grandparents. Another signature event is Reconciliation Summit, which focuses on helping grandparents experiencing estrangement or alienation along their journey to reconciliation with their families. Grandparents Academy also offers Masterclasses on many subjects by leading thought leaders and experts in the field of Grandparenting, as well as thousands of fun, printable activities available through its membership programs. My promise is that you will not be disappointed by the gathering of the best minds sharing a variety of topics that help Grandparents be the best they can be, all found at GrandparentsAcademy.com.

You will find this site also in the resources section of this book.

Knowledge and dialogue are the key ingredients to improving the Parent/Grandparent relationship challenge. Restrictions and Alienation usually develop over a long period of time. What if we look at the fundamentals of problem solving. The three most important elements of problem solving are Defining the problem, Coming up with solutions and Implementing those solutions. I am not suggesting it is that easy in these complex family issues but that does not mean that these fundamentals don't apply and won't be useful. I believe the excerpt from this article I quoted above and repeat here offers some clues as to a starting point of understanding for families.

In a recent AARP article I read, parents reported their top three most common areas of disagreement with Grandparents about Grandchildren. according to a new poll are; 57 percent said discipline, 44 percent said meals and snacks and 36 percent said screen time. I find this a hopeful place to start both parents and Grandparents on a path to understanding some major points of difference to home in on. It is instructive to realize that the six most significant people in a child's life operating from the best of intentions can be this far apart in these three areas.

If you are dealing with Restrictions an understanding of these three differences may go a long way to reversing the momentum towards Alienation.

At the outset of this chapter, when it comes to both restriction and alienation I must, appropriately, invoke Winston Churchill; "When you are going through hell, keep on going. Never, never, never give up."

Being restricted or even worse alienated from our Grandchildren is truly hell. It defies both Love and Logic. The craziest thing about it is that it is becoming more prevalent. For reasons I don't exactly understand there is an increase in these behaviors in some families. If understanding these reasons interests you I can direct you to look for Dr. Joshua Coleman or Racheal Haack MA MFTI (both to be found in resources). While I don't have the ability to explain the reasons, I can offer the best information from these experts, other Grandparents and what I have learned about what we can do as Grandparents to combat this rising silent epidemic of dysfunction in our extended families. Just like everything about Grandparenting there is, lately, a lot more attention being paid to some of these subjects. There is a greater access to information and support than any time in the history of Grandparenting. The message I wish to convey is **"You are not alone in this battle."** There is, finally, an army of us studying and sharing some of the things that are working best to help you in these difficult times.

There is definitely an increase in the amount of information but more importantly an uptick in the quality of information and the resources of professional help in this area.

Let's look towards HOPE in an area where most Grandparents' pain resides. In the resources section of this chapter, you will find Dr. Sue Cornbluth. She and her organization have affected reconciliation in families of up to 18 years of estrangement. In her own words:

Are you a grandparent that is being denied access to your grandchildren?

Are you blocked from having any contact with your grandchildren by your child?

Do you send emails, letters, gifts, and cards to your grandchildren but get no reply?

You are not alone. Hundreds of thousands of grandparents are experiencing this daily. Dr. Sue and her team also specialize in helping grandparents reunite with their grandchildren. Alienation/Estrangement from grandchildren is caused by estrangement or alienation from adult children. We understand how difficult this is to be separated from the people you are traditionally supposed to be close to.

Here at Dr. Sue and You we are trained to guide you back to your grandchildren through repairing your relationship with your adult children. We have successfully reunited hundreds of grandparents with their grandchildren.

More about Dr. Sue can be found in the Resource section of this chapter. The Alienated Grandparents Anonymous organization (AGA), which is now international, has affected reconciliation of up to 17 years. The founder of this organization has experienced reconciliation in her own family. This is why I adopt Mr. Churchill's doctrine of Never giving up.

Speaking of the AGA. This organization knows no bounds. They have helped innumerable Grandparents all over the world.

Alienated Grandparents Anonymous (AGA) focuses on the struggle millions of grandparents have in being part of their grandchildren's lives. AGA provides support, information, coping skills, and strategies for a hopeful reunification. Our organization helps validate the feelings of those suffering various levels of alienation. We offer suggestions on the advice of international experts who have shared their knowledge with AGA, from AGA professional surveys, and from communications with many thousands of grandparents who have been affected.

- We must be the voice of our grandchildren.
- They would not want you to give up on them.
- Who can our grandchildren turn to for help?

Your grandchildren are waiting to be with you, too!

You can find all about the AGA in the resource section of this chapter.

My own origin story as an author included my being drained of enthusiasm because of the thousands of sad seemingly unsolvable circumstances of folks dealing with restrictions and alienation when it came to their Grandchildren. That was nearly 20 years ago but I have learned and persevered to be in a position to deliver Hope to Grandparents in this unfortunate situation. I have since aligned with some remarkable people who excel at what they do. Coupled with the increase in this demographic and focused interest on Grandparenting challenges it has helped me become much better versed when it comes to these subjects.

My own personal story is that when my son and ex-daughter-in-law separated and subsequently divorced I had the divinely inspired common sense to not take sides. I did and still do see the mother of my amazing, now 19-year-old Granddaughter, as the wonderful mom she was and still is. The payoff for that approach is that I have always had unfettered access to time with my Granddaughter. While all the turmoil was heightened, I simply told my son that I was going to steer clear of taking sides to preserve my place in his daughter's life. Just this morning, while writing this book, I got a warm and wonderful text from said Granddaughter wishing me a Happy Father's day. Mission accomplished.

Not all endeavors are that smooth. When trouble comes knocking and things get really bad it helps to have someone who understands these kinds of situations. One of the pioneers as well as champions of Grandparenting, especially those that find themselves with these kinds of challenges, is a man named Richard S. Victor. He is the founder and executive director of the national nonprofit Grandparents Rights Organization. Over four decades later he is still contributing as a panelist on the upcoming Reconciliation Summit Hosted by Grandparents Academy. Richard has been recognized by his peers, mainstream media and Grandparents across the entire country for his decades of work on behalf of restricted and alienated Grandparents. His vast knowledge is distilled in this poignant quote.

"Remember, if death takes a grandparent from a grandchild, that is a tragedy, but if petty vindictiveness and hostilities within a family amputate a grandchild from their grandparents, then that is a shame."

- Richard S. Victor

Mr. Victor, an accomplished lawyer himself, and all of the credible experts in this field admonish Grandparents to avoid litigation. Stay away from the court whenever possible. As one expert, Dr Sue Cornbluth so eloquently states it; "You will not solve conflict with more conflict." Only mutual understanding will do that. It requires compassion not defensiveness.

This concise evaluation of what goes on in some of the extended families puts a fine point on this issue. This is why I spent so much time back on the new Grandparent Chapter of the extended family expansion admonishing Grandparents to be cognizant and considerate of the fact that this is now an extended family with new members that you may or may not have influence over and were not of your choosing.

I can sense your frustration if you find yourself at this juncture dealing with a family crisis and wondering what this author is talking about. The ole "You should-a, could-a been there." That is not the case. I would suggest that reflection of how things went down in these strained relationships with the parents of your Grandkids may provide a trail of clues of how to make things better. There may have been too much water over the dam to repair the relationship but if there is even a glimmer of hope I think your Grandkids deserve that you at least give it your best effort.

Restricting time with the Grandchildren is a whole different situation. This can get to be punitive and manipulative. I have spoken to many Grandparents who feel that they have to do certain things before they get to see the Grandkids. Things like babysitting at a moment's notice. Some Grandparents even express the need to help their kids and in-laws financially in order to get time with the Grandkids.

I can understand restricting access to Grandparents when the Grandparents are bad actors. What I don't understand is when restricting access crosses over into manipulation territory. Some are precipitated by deteriorating relations with in-laws, but some are just opportunistic by nature. I wish it wasn't so but it happens more often than you would think. This is especially true if one or both parents are involved in drugs, or any other type of criminal activity. This is a sad and frustrating circumstance, but I do think it is important that you recognize it for what it is.

Another area of restriction occurs when there is a divorce. This is complicated by a protracted custody battle. The complications are even more severe if the husband is not paying Child Support. Often the Daughter-in-law will not let the kids visit the Grandparents if the Father is going to be present at the time of the visit. You may not be open to it but this is a solvable issue. Each of these circumstances dictates what you as a Grandparent must do if you wish to maintain contact with your Grandchildren. The importance of these considerations is that they will statistically occur in one half of the families in America. You can hope for a better outcome, IF this happens, but you will be wise to prepare for WHEN.

No matter the circumstances, if the relationship is severely strained and deteriorated it is advisable to get some professional help to guide you through. Several of the folks in the resources listed below will gladly help you find the right person to aid you. If it is not them, they have remarkable resources to refer you to. Not all family law practitioners are well versed in this area of the law and/or mediation in these cases. All of the resources listed here are people of integrity and they have a genuine concern for the Grandchildren as well as the Grandparent.

Chapter 7

SUMMARY OF CARING ABOUT YOUR GRANCHILDREN

"Keep me away from the wisdom which does not cry, the philosophy which does not laugh, and the greatness which does not bow before children."

- Khalil Gibran

First and foremost, you as a Grandparent have to know who you are and how you choose to operate in the context of this new extended family. Next, as best you can, figure out what all the stakeholders in your extended family are looking for. It is clear that the less you make this about fairness and the more strategic you are the better the outcome you will have.

The foundation that you build under your Lasting Meaningful Connections with your Grandchildren starts before your first Grandchild is born. You further strengthen that foundation by partnering with the parents of your Grandchildren at every opportunity. Your role as Parent enhancer goes a long way to accomplishing a long and happy relationship with your Grandkids.

This is a Grandparenting existential truth; Your new Grandchild and each subsequent Grandchild is in the hands of their parents. I propose an 11th

"Grandparent commandment"; "Thou shalt honor thy Grandchildren's Mother and Father." For this evolution of your family to be fruitful you must make it more about the parents and the Grandchild and less about you.

Your family is expanded to include more people, however they might not all have your understanding of how that family can function. When possible, meeting each person where they are goes a long way.This is where the rubber hits the road. Keep your Grandchildren's best interest top of mind.

Become a close observer of your Grandkids and meet them at the crossroads of, their interests and their interests, at any point in their growth. As you probably already know, this is an ever more rapidly changing landscape. Asking them and/or their parents is your best source for information. Next is their social media activity. Ask them to show you the way, most will gladly teach you.

Remember they will remember how you make them feel much more that what you tell them.

This is also true for what you buy them. Be thoughtful and careful in your gift giving to your Grandchildren. Same goes with their consequences. Don't try to do too much for them, rather support them in doing for themselves. Constant rescue becomes enabling.

If you are restricted or alienated from your Grandchildren never give up hope. Even if it is years later the message that you never stopped loving them is transformational. In the interim keep trying. If possible, remember that compassion is the antidote to conflict, not defensiveness.

Chapter 8

RESOURCES

Aaron Larsen
Grandparents Academy. https://www.grandparentsacademy.com/

This is the most current and accurate source for information to enhance your experience as a Grandparent. Founded and run by Aaron Larsen. It is also a resource of resources and learning about many areas of Grandparenting by the best in the business of helping Grandparents.

Dee Dee Moore
More Than Grand. https://www.morethangrand.com/

This is a great place for information, especially for new Grandparents. Founded and run by Dee Dee Moore. You will find good and current information about Grandparenting

Dr. Kerry Byrne
https://thelongdistancegrandparent.com/

This is the best site for staying in touch with your distant Grandkids. Founded and run by Dr. Kerry Byrne. She is innovative in communicating with your

Grandkids that live a distance away from you as well as creative about what to do when you go to visit them.

Greg Payne
The Cool Grandpa. https://cool-grandpa.us/

Grandpas sometimes get forgotten. Not now. Founded and run by Greg Payne who will help you be current on what is up with Grandfathers. Greg hosts a weekly podcast that has excellent guests and information.

Dr. Sue Cornbluth
Dr. Sue and You. https://www.drsueandyou.com/

She is a certified parental expert, author, coach, etc. Drsueandyou.com Her strength is in The power of compassion in conflict.

Alienated Grandparents Anonymous, Inc.
AGA, Inc. https://www.alienatedgrandparentsanonymous.com/

An International Organization, AGA focuses on the struggle millions of Grandparents have in being part of their Grandchildren's lives.

Dr. Joshua Coleman
Joshua Coleman, Ph.D https://www.drjoshuacoleman.com/

His book is titled "THE RULES OF ESTRANGEMENT"
He is an expert in the field of adult estrangement.

Rachael Haack MA MFTI
Origins and Counselling. https://www.originscounselingnv.com

Origins Counseling invites you to a supportive, confidential space to remove the mask and be honest. They recognize that successful, modern mental health treatment is inextricably linked to our most fundamental needs.

AARP
https://www.aarp.org/

This site has some good articles and chat groups about Grandparenting.

Richard S. Victor, PLLC
https://www.richardsvictor.com/

Richard is THE pioneer of Grandparents rights and finding ways to reconciliation for families. He is the founder of Grandparents Rights Organization; https://www.grandparentsrights.org/

Focus on the Family
https://www.focusonthefamily.com/

Focus on the Family also features information about Grandparenting.

Legacy Coalition
https://legacycoalition.com/

Legacy Coalition is a Christion Grandparents organization.

Companion site to this book: https://www.caringgrandparents.com/

- It is the Mission of this site to elevate the bond of Caring Grandparents with their Grandchildren to even more meaningful connections. This can be achieved by partnering with their parents as well as education through stories and examples of things that are currently working between Grandparents and their Grandchildren in the 21st Century.

- In recognition of the evolving times, it is increasingly important to gain insight into the social, educational, and spiritual well-being of our grandchildren. As we improve our understanding of Grandparents' Rights and Responsibilities, we will enhance the well-being of our grandchildren, children, and the entire extended family.

- As our Grandkids grow, we will have the tools to expand our knowledge of where they are and stay connected in meaningful ways.

PART 2

Grandparents Caring FOR Grandchildren

Chapter 1

STEPPING UP

"The world's battlefields have been in the heart chiefly, more heroism has been displayed in the household and the closet, than on the memorable battlefields in history."

- Henry Ward Beecher

They number over 2.5 million households serving some 8 million children in need according to the United States Census. This is a group of Grandparents who thought they were past the phase of raising children in their homes. They made elaborate plans and saved for years to realize the glory of this time in their lives. They planned and spoke of their dreams of freedom and reward for having done their level best to raise their children. Plans are in place to sell the house and buy a much smaller one for just the two of them. Some have already purchased the RV they will call home for months each year as they go to those places they couldn't afford with all of the kids. Now, instead of those extra bedrooms being turned into an office and a sewing room they now have bunk beds, kids toys and a small desk for school study. Many Grandparents had already downsized and moved to adult communities or smaller condo units. They face the challenge of having to move to accommodate their Grandchildren. This transition back to parenthood often happens on the spur of the moment with a phone call or a visit from a social worker from Child Protective Services. The announcement is that a family tragedy has occurred, and the Grandparents are called on to clean up the mess. No time to even be disappointed. No time for grief. That all comes later when the dust of this family crisis settles. For now, there are just these needy, confused, often damaged, scarred, and scared Grandchildren to rescue.

Often there is no time for the Grandparents to research. There is no understanding that raising a child to age 18 in today's world costs about a quarter of a million dollars. That is pre-college cost. There is no time to find out that the Grandparents will not be socially embraced with Grandkids in tow by most of their present social circle. Many talk about feeling socially isolated. They don't yet realize that the discipline system that worked with their own kids may be far from what will work with emotionally scarred children that may act out their own fears and anger about being abandoned. This usually requires therapy appointments for them and you to be added to your schedule. Grandparents in this shocked state haven't considered the legal and custodial mambo jumbo that goes along with these new "Stepchildren" that have entered their lives.

I would be remiss if I didn't raise the possibility that you will be raising a child that comes with a tremendous amount of psychological baggage. Some were born to drug addled mothers; Some have suffered abuse and neglect that has scarred them deeply. Some will act out with violent anger. These are seldom your quiet, well-behaved Grandkids that you remember before their family tragedy.

There isn't time for you to consider your own health/energy challenges either. I won't belabor the list but there will be more things added as time goes on.

The affected Grandparents vary widely in their personal circumstances, their economic situations, their prior involvement with their Grandkids, their proximity to retirement, etc.

Stepping up to care for your Grandchild or Grandchildren changes everything regardless of your age, your willingness, your station in life, etc. You are right to say to yourself, I already did this, why do I have to start all over again at my age?

The alarming news is that these situations have just gone through a doubling in the past several years. There has been a triple whammy recently. The increase in Grandparents caring for their Grandchildren has doubled due to the Opioid Crisis, Covid and the ensuing Mental Health Crisis among young people.

Fortunately, back in 1986 a couple of organizations anticipated this great need. They were The National Council on Aging and The Child Welfare League of America; They formed the now flourishing Generations United organization (Generations United.org). This organization has since been joined by The Child Defense Fund and The AARP to produce a force whose sole purpose is to "Improve the life of children'." They have three major focal thrusts. 1) High Quality Intergenerational Programs, 2) Intergenerational use of Spaces and Places and 3) Grandfamilies and Intergenerational use of Households. This is the organization that coined the term Grandfamilies. Generations United is, hands down, the ultimate, while not the only, resource of a plethora of programs that support Grandparents raising Grandchildren. You will also hear some people refer to caring for your Grandchildren as Kinship Care.

Others that are stepping up are organizations like your local YMCA that may host a "Grandparents Raising Grandchildren" program as they do here in Wilmington NC.

In recent years there has been an uptick in support for Grandparents Raising Grandchildren that mirrors the increase in those having to step in and assume this important and life-changing role as caregivers for these little ones.

I invite you to ride along with me as I reveal some of these Grandparents stories. The outcomes are not all gloom and doom, but the burden is real and significant in all cases. I use the word burden because in almost every case these Grandparents have been rerouted from their own Hopes and Dreams for their later years of life.

Let me offer you a glimpse into some of the lives of Grandparents who, willingly or not, have taken up the mantle of raising their Grandchildren. I say willingly or not because the circumstances that have precipitated this need span the spectrum from teen pregnancy to tragedy out of the blue, to Grandparents who willingly take up this task.

One such story has to do with me. To this day I call this 50 something year old beautiful Mom, Puddle. It was over a half century ago. Back then my dear friends, Patty and Dean, and I were inseparable. A good illustration of that is that we can't remember whether it was me that took Patty to the hospital to have her first daughter and Dean that brought her home or was it Dean that took her and me that brought her home. Let it suffice to say that we were fast friends and that has not changed over the past 60 years. I do remember that Dean took Patty to the hospital to have their second daughter and I was the one to pick them up to bring them home. The reason I remember that is that Patty insisted on driving, and I got to hold my future

God daughter, Suzy, while she cried all the way home. Relax, this was over 60 years ago. We didn't even know what a car seat was back then.

Fast forward to when their first child, Teresa, was 15. She came home one day to announce that she was pregnant. This was not a good day in their very meager household. Tears and maybe a bit of shouting and pacing ensued. After the fury settled down the decision was made that Teresa would carry this baby full term and the family would figure a way to make it work. This time stands out clearly to me because Dean asked me to see if he could work a second job at the gas station where I worked. He did and the upside was that I got to spend an extra day each week hanging out with my buddy Dean. As time progressed and this little girl began to show signs of her pregnancy we showed her no mercy. We picked on her incessantly as she leaned back more and more when she walked and had trouble getting up out of a chair. I will never understand why little ladies get sooooooo big when they are pregnant. At any rate we made it through, and she had, possibly, the most beautiful girl ever born to that point in time. She was named Kerry. But hold on, that name didn't last long. I first got to meet this stunning miracle one Saturday morning when she was about a week old. I stopped by the house to pick up Dean for our day at the gas station and Grandma Patty held up this tiny little lady and said "Neil, I would like you to meet Kerry." I took her from Patty and cradled her head in my hand and put her up to my shoulder right gently and in no time at all, she proceeded to pee on my uniform shirt. We all laughed and as I handed her back to Grandma I said, "I christen this child Puddle".

I told that story, with Kerry's permission, at her Grandpa Dean's funeral and then the entire family finally understood why I have always called her, Puddle.

I insert some warmth and levity into a story that actually played out a bit differently. As it turned out Grandma and Grandpa, through considerable emotional and financial challenges, went on to raise Puddle to be a still beautiful, Loving and Lovable lady. There were some tough times both financially and with their daughter making some horrendous choices in her life. Teresa continued to spiral and this caused even more strain on the entire family as well as me. I was and still am a bonus Dad to Teresa. The good news is that Puddle is now a wonderful Mom and a force for good in their family and the world around her. Good job Grandma Patty and Grandpa Dean.

This story took place over 60 years ago. I can tell you that there was NO support for Grandma Patty and Grandpa Dean back then. They stepped up out of pure Love and a conviction of doing the right thing. Looking back at what they had to sacrifice to take in this precious baby and the fact that they raised her to be such a Loving and Lovable woman stretches the bounds of the word admiration. Grandma Patty is still a prized friend of mine as is "Puddle". The glorious thing is that all these years later I still get an enthusiastic hug from Puddle's Mom Teresa each time I see her.

That was then and this is now. Today's stories are hard to cloak in warmth and levity. Take my friends Bill and Barbara. A couple in their late 50s. He is an electrical engineer, and she was an inferior designer. They lived in a nice Midwest home that was becoming too large for the two of them since both of their children had long ago married and moved away from their hometown. Their son, Chad had twin 9-year-old boys that looked forward to coming for a week each summer to get spoiled by Grandma and Grandpa. Bill and Barb would spend either Thanksgiving or Christmas at the boys house each year. In between were the weekly phone and now Zoom calls with Chad and tribe. These two boys thought their Grandpa hung the moon.

The alternating holidays were spent with their daughter Britney's family who lived closer. Britney was the older of the two siblings and had been the rebel of the family. She and her then boyfriend ran away when they were teens and only returned when she got pregnant, and they needed to settle down. They returned and stayed with Bill and Barb for several months until they could get their own place. Things seemed to settle down in the coming years. Tom got a job at an Auto Parts/Mechanics shop in a town about 45 minutes away. They subsequently had two additional children. Bill and Barb did what they could to welcome Britney's husband Tom into the family, but he was a bit of a loaner and not as sociable as the rest of the family. Bill is a bit of a gregarious guy and even he had trouble connecting with Tom over the past 10 years. Barb often shared with Bill that she was worried and sensed that Britney was becoming more distant and was hiding how things were actually going. Both Barb and Bill reached out to her but still tried not to meddle. They let her know they were there if there was anything they could do. Then they got the call that Britney was in the emergency room from a fall down the rear stairs of their home. She was really banged up but was a bit distant when Mom and Dad went to the hospital to see how she was. Tom was still sullen and quiet. For some time after that incident Barb tried to reach out again but Britney was not very responsive. They skipped Thanksgiving that year at Britney's request. She also didn't call as much. A couple of months later Britney called her Mom at work and asked if she could bring the kids and come over and talk that evening. She asked if Grandpa could take the kids out for the evening so Mom and daughter could have some time to talk. This obviously worried Barb and then Bill but they said sure.

That evening, while Grandpa plied the three Grandkids, Sue 9, Jason 6 and Brett 3, with ice cream and a Disney movie, Britney poured out to her mother what she had already suspected. There was no fall down the stairs, Tom came home hammered that evening and they argued. It turned violent and that is where the injuries came from. She said she wanted to leave Tom and move home, but she was afraid that would precipitate more violence. Britney had seen the rage build in Tom over the years and had come to fear it. There were other near misses over the years but none as bad as the emergency room event. Barb gently guided Britney through talking this out. By the end of the evening Britney had decided to return home with the kids and try to get Tom to go for counseling. A couple of days later when Britney got up the nerve to broach the subject with Tom it went badly. Tom flew into a rage that scared Britney and the kids. Tom stormed out of the house. Britney, wisely, packed up the kids and headed for Bill and Barb's house. Later that night Tom came banging on the front door demanding to talk with his wife. Bill, who is a substantial guy, tried to calm Tom. His son-in-law, who was bolstered by alcohol was not hearing Bill. Barb, in the other room, became concerned and called the police. They came, ordered Tom to leave and the family tried to settle the kids and get some sleep. The next day while Tom was at work Britney and Barb returned to retrieve enough clothes and stuff for her and the kids to stay with Grandma and Grandpa. A few evenings later the drunken Tom returned, and the same scene played out with the police telling him to leave. The next day Britney applied for it and was granted a restraining order against Tom.

Two weeks went by without incident. One Tuesday at lunchtime Barb gets a frantic call from her daughter that Tom was in the house and waving a gun around. Barb called the police and then Bill. Barb was shaken so Bill picked her up from work and they raced home. When they arrived, their front yard was cordoned off with crime tape, the driveway was filled with police cars and the sidewalk was lined with curious neighbors. Bill approached one of the officers and asked what was going on. He was told that they could not go in. Bill protested vehemently that this was their house and that was their family in there. The police captain came over and explained that their daughter was okay, but their 6-year-old grandson had been shot but was expected to be okay. He was being transported to the nearby hospital. Once again Bill asserted that this was his house and his family. The captain told him that their home was an active crime scene, and no one was allowed in except law enforcement. He assured them both that they would be allowed back in when the police sorted all of this out. In the meantime, they saw their son-in-law being led, in handcuffs, to a police cruiser and being taken to jail. Their daughter had gone to the hospital with her 6-year-old son Jason and social services had come to look after Sue and Brett.

Can you imagine the fear and frustration of these two loving Grandparents, coming home to this horrific chaos and then having to stand there helpless to do anything?

Bill decided to head to the hospital to be with Britney and Jason while Barb stayed to talk with the Social Services lady when she finally emerged from the crime scene. Barb asked Bill to give her a call on her cell when he found out what had happened from Britney. That call came about a half hour later. It seems that around noon Tom came banging on the front door and Britney was too scared to open it. He then went around the back and one of the sliding glass doors was unlocked. He entered to find Britney, Sue, Jason and Brett cowering in the corner of Jason and Brett's bedroom. He began to rage and wave a gun around. He threatened to kill Britney if she didn't bring the kids home. This went on for a few minutes and then he fired the gun past Britney to scare her. The bullet hit Jason in the leg and panic set in. They all came to help Jason at the same time. Sue, showing a maturity beyond her 9 years, ran out of the room and called the police while Britney and Tom got towels to help with the bleeding from Jason's leg.

When the police neared with sirens blaring Tom panicked and started for the back door, he had come in. By now some neighbors heard the commotion and stopped Tom and held him there in the backyard. Fortunately, he had dropped the gun upstairs during the flurry of activity. Sue let the police in the front door and the neighbors brought Tom around the side to other waiting police. The ambulance arrived shortly after that and took Jason and his Mom to the hospital. Bill reported that the wound, while serious, was not life threatening.

Just after the call from Bill the Social Services lady emerged with the kids. Barb got to hug her precious Grandkids for the first time after standing in the front yard for almost an hour. She had to follow the Social Service lady to the police station to retrieve her Grandkids. They said that was the procedure, so she complied. It was into the evening before all the paperwork and interviews were completed. Bill stayed with Britney who would not leave the side of her son that evening.

It is only fair to you the reader that I unwind this story that happened some 5 years ago now. Jason recovered physically but the ongoing psychological trauma still haunts everyone involved. One blessing in all of this yucky stuff is that Bill and Barb belong to a loving faith community and one of their friends from church was able to find a psychologist that specializes in this specific type of parental violence against a child. This connection has helped in a couple of ways. Jason, now 11, is showing signs of healing this tremendous trauma and the community has raised the considerable funds to pay for this care which would have bankrupted the family. The psychologist is also including the entire family, including the Grandparents, in this care as well.

Tom was obviously convicted for his crimes and was paroled after two years. Britney has shown signs of improvement but not to the extent that she is able to return to her role as a single Mom. They all still live with Bill and Barb. It became necessary for the Grandparents to adopt the kids for various reasons. To do this Tom had to relinquish his parental rights. Here is the hard pill to swallow. In order for this to occur Bill and Barb had to agree that he gets scheduled supervised visits with the three kids at the psychologist's office. I know it stinks but that is the law. I once wrote that sometimes Logic and Law are strange bedfellows.

Let me conclude this story by telling you that the level of Caring and the Faith that it took for Bill and Barb to surrender their lives to these circumstances and rebuild the lives of all concerned as best they can show Grandparenting at its highest and most loving level. Thankfully, because of who they are, they started with some resources of their own as well as they managed to garner continued support and help from a loving faith community. Not all Grandparents are so blessed.

I wish I could say that this is the only story that was the product of mind-boggling violence but that would not be true.

Now onto an uplifting story. When it comes to Grandparents there are always stories of Love and Hope.

Now I want to share my favorite, albeit unique Grandparenting story with a tremendous outcome.

Another of my friends endured all kinds of inexplicable setbacks yet managed to make a silk purse out of a sow's ear.

Meet my friend Jim. He is the very rare paternal Grandfather who found himself in a position as savior to two young Grandsons. Jim was enjoying a fruitful life in spite of a midlife divorce. He maintained a strong relationship with his son James, his wife Brenda and his two young Grandsons Jake and Josh. It was about this time that Jim met and got remarried to a wonderful lady named Jenny. Within days of their wedding tragedy struck when Jim's son James became deathly ill and shortly thereafter passed away from his illness. This left Jim's grieving young daughter-in-law as a single mom with a 1- and 3-year-old to care for. Jim and Jenny jumped into action to help her through in any way possible. They spent long hours just being present to Brenda and along with her mom Grammy looked after the boys to give Brenda time to grieve. Brenda knew all too well what it was like to lose a dad early in life. She was grateful to have her mom close by.

As things returned to the new normal Brenda wanted/needed to return to work so Grammy moved in with them to look after the boys. They tried to make as much of a family as possible. Just two years later these poor little 4- and 6-year-old boys also lost their mother in a car wreck. She was hit, head on by a drunk driver on her way home from work one evening. Grammy, along with a lot of help from Jim and Jenny tried to make a home for the boys. She was a doting and loving Grammy and the boys seemed to feel very loved. They all made the best life possible after another tragedy. Jim and Jenny would have the boys over for overnighters to give Grammy space to grieve and heal as well. What became a group effort was the best for all concerned. After a year of this arrangement Grammy had to go into the hospital for some surgery. When she came home, she just didn't bounce back the way the doctors expected. It became obvious that she was unable to care for the boys.

At this Jim prayed and consulted with his new wife Jenny as to what could be done. Jenny didn't hesitate, she told Jim that she had grown to love her Grandsons and they committed to take them in. They applied and received the proper credentials to become the boys' guardians and became a family of 4. Grammy never recovered and passed away a few years after her daughter. One has to wonder if she didn't die of a broken heart.

Jim and Jenny immediately adopted Jake and Josh and continued to raise them. I say this is rare for a paternal Grandpa to adopt his Grandsons. As a matter of fact, I know of no other situation where this is the case.

As time went on it was kind of cute, the boys began to call Jenny Mom which indicates they felt very accepted by her and Jim. Fast forward they are now in their 20s. They have grown into wonderful, productive young men who continually shower gratitude on their "Mom and Dad/Grandma and Granddad". My hat is off to these stellar Grandparents.

Now you know why it is my favorite Grandparents Raising Grandchildren story.

I use these three stories to illustrate how some of the millions of Caring Grandparents find themselves derailed from their own plans through no actions of their own and are thrust into a brand new, sometimes scary and always difficult, but essential role they had not chosen. No matter the path to this juncture, the reality is that life in these and all Grandparents Raising Grandchildren's lives is changed forever.

"It is what you do next that counts"
From the TV show "Blue Bloods"

I think the use of these stories does a better job of illustrating how "Life happens" than my trying to pontificate on the potential for potholes in the road to retirement for some Grandparents.

Get ready for another story that is even more challenging, more frustrating and in many ways even sadder than the previous three.

Bobby and his sweetheart Chelsea met and fell madly in love as high school juniors. They went to senior prom together and got married right after they graduated. Bobby went to work for his Uncle Jack building houses, one at a time, there in their small town and Chelsea landed a job at the corner convenience store. They borrowed a few dollars from their parents and got their own apartment and a beat-up old car. Bobby didn't need a car since his Uncle Jack picked him up each morning on his way to work.

Almost on cue, near their first anniversary this bright-eyed miracle that they named Sue was born. Even though money was tight they decided that Chelsea would be a stay-at-home Mom for at least the first 6 months. After that Celsea's Mom and her sister Jill, who had a one-year-old, would assume the daytime care of Sue. It was three years before Sue had a brother that was named Bobby Jr. This scenario played out pretty well like when Sue was born since Chelsea's sister Jill was still a stay-at-home Mom.

With the addition of Bobby Jr., the apartment space became smaller and smaller. Bobby had saved some money, so he bought a lot near his parents' there in town and with some help from Uncle Jack he began to build their house. Because of money and time constraints it took him almost a year to build their house.

Amazingly this is where Bobby's commitment to family shined the brightest. With this mammoth task ahead of him he decided the first thing he would build was a giant Jungle Jim, slide and swings in the backyard so his kids could be entertained while he toiled to build them a home. They shuttled back and forth between the building site and Grandma and Grandpa's house just down the block. They didn't even have to cross any streets.

Further signs of what a family man Bobby was, he next built the patio, complete with barbeque pit and rear screen enclosed porch so Chelsea had a comfortable place to observe the kids at play. It was only then that he commenced to build the rest of the house.

As you can imagine the new housewarming party was quite the affair with family, church community and friends galore. That back yard was filled to overflowing. Their life was starting to take shape.

Chelsea was able to cut back to part time and began to make their new house a warm and inviting home. Meanwhile Bobby was learning and taking on more responsibilities at work. Uncle Jack was now in his early 60s and began to talk about retiring. Since Bobby was more like a partner than an employee the two of them laid out a plan for Bobby to buy out Uncle Jack over the next 5 years. During this time Sue and Bobby Jr. were gifted a new baby sister, Lily.

As a family of 5 now, Bobby kept his nose to the grindstone. Uncle Jack began to turn over the reins even more to him in the coming years. He also increased his pay enough for him to afford the buyout and for Chelsea to be a full time stay at home Mom. Bobby had to spend a few extra hours a week to get everything done but he didn't seem to mind.

About 2 ½ years into the 5-year plan Jack went into the hospital for some stomach surgery. Turns out they found cancer, and they told Jack two things.

One is that he would not be able to do the physical work he had been doing. The second was even more devastating, the cancer had metastasized, and they were not sure what his future looked like. He took it hard, but Bobby told him not to worry a bit about the business. He had this. He was ready and would be able to support Uncle Jack by continuing the buyout even though he would not have Jack to lean on. He fully knew that this would add a few more hours a week but was up for the task. Chelsea was on board also.

Uncle Jack lasted a year but had many good days during that time right up until near the end. Bobby kept his word even after Jack was gone, he finished the payout without fail to his widow, Aunt Beth.

She was so grateful and impressed that Bobby had managed to grow the business out of sheer effort and determination. This required some extra hours and a few Saturdays, but Bobby kept his eye on the future of his family. With kids now 10, 7 and 5 he had quite the responsibility, but he wore it well. His entire life was based around his family. Over the next 4 years Bobby began to be recognized by the business community for his good work, fine houses and community involvement. Sue would be off to high school. Bobby Jr. was doing well in school as was Lily.

At first Chelsea would drive Sue the 20 minutes to the new high school one town over, while Bobby dropped the other two off at their school. It didn't take long for Sue to want to ride the bus with her friends. Chelsea sort of welcomed this so she could take the little ones to school and Bobby could leave earlier to get ahead of his crew at work. All seemed to work out well.

It was late in Sue's freshman year. While she was at school her Mom walked into her room one morning to collect the dirty clothes for laundry day and she smelled a weird odor that she had never noticed before. As Chelsea later learned marijuana smell clings to wools and bedclothes more than any other fabric. She also learned that the person smoking it gets used to the smell and doesn't realize how poignant the smell is getting. Chelsea called Bobby at work, and they decided that a prayer meeting that evening with Sue was appropriate. Sue denies knowing what they were talking about and begins to show an attitude they haven't seen before. They don't tear through her room, instead, they give her a chance to get rid of anything she has hidden but that she has lost any future privilege of privacy in her room. Things finally calmed down in a few days and her parents became more vigilant. One of the things they did was to check with the school to be sure she was attending each day. Turns out she had missed a few days. She was grounded. More attitude so her phone was taken away.

Things stayed tense throughout the summer. They later found that one of her so-called friends at school had gotten her another phone. It was early in her sophomore year that she went to school one day and didn't return that afternoon. Panic, search and more panic. Three days later they found her about two hours away with a 17-year-old guy that was a junior at her school.

Things remained like this. Trusting Sue was no longer an option for her parents. She ran away two more times that year and the third time she came home pregnant and had a whole lot more attitude. This time the guy was 20 years old, and he went to jail.

It became a constant battle with her sneaking out even while she was pregnant. It became obvious that both drugs and alcohol were involved. She had her baby Laurie early that summer. This expanded their family to 6.

After she brought Laurie home Sue feigned interest but didn't have the maturity nor the inclination to care for her new baby. Sue's parents did what they could to keep the peace in the family, but Sue's belligerence affected everyone in the house. She returned to school that year and things seemed a bit better except for the attitude she brought home each day. She only got caught slipping out two times that year and only once during her entire senior year. Chelsea worked hard to teach Sue how to care for her daughter and sometimes Sue showed signs of becoming a pretty good Mom.

Just prior to graduation Sue went missing for a few days. They found her and she returned home, this time with a bit of remorse. She stayed, graduated and seemed to be taking to this role as a mom. A few months after Laurie's 4th birthday Sue disappeared with a 28-year-old guy and vanished for a few months. When they finally found her, they could do nothing. She was now 18 and she let them know in her defiant tone, that she had no intention of coming back home.

Bobby and Chelsea saw no alternative so they petitioned the court for Custody of Laurie so they could properly care for her in medical situations, enroll her in pre-school, etc. The court granted guardianship since Sue was so young and, in the event, she returned the court would have options.

The law will return a child to its birth mother if she shows any signs of wanting custody back.

I tell this long story to inform Grandparents of how brutal this kind of Caring Grandparent journey can be. I won't belabor this story any further except to say that this coming back and taking Laurie happened three more times in the ensuing 7 years. Each time Sue ran again, Grandma and Grandpa were tasked with picking up the pieces. Many nights they had to sit on the side of Laurie's bed trying to explain to a sad, growing young child that Mommy would not be home that night, and then another night, etc. This scene breaks my heart the most.

Tragically, one night both Booby and Chelsea had to sit on the side of Laurie's bed but this time to tell this sobbing 11-year-old girl that her Mommy would not be coming back, ever. Sue had died of an overdose this time.

It was only then that these grieving, Loving Grandparents could petition the court and, since the biological father didn't show up, they received an order that allowed them to adopt Laurie as their own.

This kind of story plays out all too often with families. The only silver lining is that there are Grandparents willing to step up and let these little ones know that they are dearly Loved and will be cared for.

As in all Loving families, some good came of all this chaos. Bobby Jr., admitted to trying pot once and decided never again and Lilly pledged to stay clear of both drugs and alcohol. The jury is still out on Laurie, but she has grown to be a wonderful, popular and productive young lady. Both Bobby and Chelsea are proud parents and extraordinary Caring Grandparents.

.

Chapter 2

THE THREE D's – Drugs, Desertion, and Detention

"It's not uncool to worry about people who seem like they're going on the wrong path. There's nothing cool about being self-destructive."

- Patti Smith

While usually not mutually exclusive, each of these three D's account for the vast majority of what causes Grandparents to reroute their lives on behalf of their Grandkids.

DRUGS

You will have to excuse my rage here, but this is primarily the result of one greedy family and their entire downline supply chain that knowingly decided to profit off the backs of not only young people but their entire families including our beloved Grandchildren. They are as bad as the cartels. Outrage is the only appropriate response.

130 people a day die from overdoses according to the Health Resources and Service Administration. All of this for the profit of one family and their downline supply chain that are so far getting away with it. I have stated

elsewhere in this book that Logic and Law are strange bedfellows, but this is one case where my personal response is "shame on the courts, defense attorneys and the perpetrators."

Sermon over.

In some of my interviews with addiction experts and addicts I am perplexed by what I have heard. These are not mean, vindictive, violent people. They are by and large folks that were pretty good citizens of society that still want to be pretty good citizens of society that are caught in a downward spiral of chemical destruction that is ever so difficult to get out of. Just like Sue, the daughter of Bobby and Chelsea in the earlier story. She repeatedly returned home with the intention of becoming the mother she wanted to be, only to fall prey to her addiction once more.

I am not in favor of granting all addicts victimhood. I am not in favor of no accountability for the addicted, I am however in favor of finding a way that works rather than this ongoing spiral of profit and failure, profit and failure.

In the US we have identified by census at least 2.5 million Grandparents who have stepped up to care for their Grandchildren. At some point we run out of motivated, Caring Grandparents and then what? What do we do with the Grandchildren affected by this crisis? We can't throw them away.

As Caring Grandparents, we are duty bound to be creative in our thinking. I am a proponent of preemptive actions. I am pretty sure the answers are not easy and/or obvious but no matter how difficult the price of watching our children and Grandchildren suffer so greatly is way too high.

Instead of more ranting let me proffer one possible way of looking at this

Opioid Crisis. A mid-west University, (not sure of the school but that is not as important as what they learned), did a study of rats. They put them in a regular plain cage and had one bottle feed them water, the other water laced with drugs. In short order the rats went for the drugs to their own demise. They then put some rats in a cage that had things like wheels, slides, ladders, etc. A regular ole rat park. They included the same two bottles, one with drugs and one without. With very few exceptions the rats opted for the bottle with just water. The rats flourish when able to do what rats do. I ask you. Is there a clue here? I am not an expert, but I do believe that with different thinking we can get different outcomes.

Let's look at this challenge from a different angle. "The War on Drugs". Richard Nixon declared this war 53 years ago. Here is a response from just one state.

Consider this in an article by BRETT MONTEGUE.

"In Mississippi, our drug laws have often fallen in simultaneous step with the War on Drugs. Yet, drug use and overdose rates are increasing and thousands of families have a loved one currently incarcerated on a non-violent drug charge in the Mississippi prison system."

Again, I am not all that concerned with how we solve this problem, just that we do. I call on Grandparents to consider how you can impact this issue. It starts with what you do as a Caring Grandparent. You are not "THE" preventative force in your Grandkids lives but you are a powerful force all the same.

DESERTION

Grit, determination, dedication, stick-to- itiveness, perseverance, etc. are all based on one thing.... Hope.

I have studied the stories of many good and great leaders in both business and politics. One theme rises to the top in so many stories. They refused to give up.

Test me on this; Fred Smith of FedEx, Alexander Hamilton, Louis Armstrong, Job, Abraham Lincoln, Elon Musk with SpaceX, Jack Canfield (Chicken Soup guy), Tony Robbins, George Washington Carver, et al.

I rest my case. It would be fair for you to ask where I am going with this. When it comes to Grandparents raising their Grandchildren I have seen a pattern. The parents that abandon their responsibilities for their children lack Hope. This sometimes manifests itself because they are guilt ridden and/or are strung out on some drug or another. I believe there is only one unforgivable sin and that is despair. I don't know if I can defend that theologically but if there is no Hope there is no redemption.

My approach to helping people is to foster Hope. Back when my own children were small, I used to read to them from the book "There is Hope for the Flowers". By Trina Paulus

A note from the author of that book: "Somehow, we each have to understand, that uncomfortable as it may feel, in some way you and I were meant for this time. Regardless of the quotidian events that are swirling around us, some with the dubious ability to divide rather than unite—age, sex, class, religion, country, politics, the scourge of a present- and post-

COVID world—we are grateful that Hope, and everything it stands for, was given to us as gift."

It is also my belief that creating Hope in our own Children and Grandchildren is a Superpower that we can exercise. If we missed it in our own children, it is not too late to do what we can to instill it in our Grandchildren.

DETENTION

When one or both parents spend time detained it may very well fall on us to keep the home fires burning for our Grandchildren until the parents get out of jail. If it is the father that is in jail the mother of our Grandkids will need exceptional support. This may include taking her back into your home for a period of time. It may also include financial subsidizing to prevent things like losing her home and further complicating the post incarceration recovery of the family unit. If it is the mother, it is a long shot that the father will step up. If he does, then like-kind supplemental care will help keep the family unit intact.

These are difficult times for all concerned and the amount of contribution will differ by the circumstances. Two very important considerations are the psychological impact on all the stakeholders and the post incarceration difficulties with things like employment, adjustment to life outside of the jail system, etc.

Chapter 3

PRACTICAL CONSIDERATIONS

"If you hold a cat by the tail, you learn things you cannot learn any other way."

- Mark Twain

I mentioned in Part 1 of this book that becoming a Grandparent and Caring ABOUT your grandchildren doesn't just happen. You gain so much by being intentional about it. Becoming a Grandparent that is raising Grandchildren requires a lot of intentionality and consideration in many areas. Some of them you probably have already thought about but some may surprise you.

Since each case is different, I hope to offer you a thorough list of things to consider making this transition smoother and more beneficial for all concerned. Things are different if this transition is thrust upon you out of nowhere or if you see this coming and have time to plan. I will suggest things in an order that addresses urgency rather than importance. All these considerations are important but not necessarily urgent.

When my Granddaughter was in school my son included me on the list of authorized adults to pick her up. This is a good preemptive item that benefits everyone. If your role changes due to an unexpected event this is one area, you don't have to worry about. Some Grandparents have the needed Medical authority if the Grandkids come to visit for any period of time. Once again this takes care of that need ahead of time. If you don't have this it is a difficult, but not always impossible hoop to jump through in case of an urgent need or unexpected event that causes you to step into the role of caregiver.

No matter how you become a Grandparent raising your Grandchildren you will need to seek court approval to become their legal guardian to make many decisions on their behalf. If one or both parents are still alive guardianship is probably as far as the courts will go at first.

It is handy to have a list of the children's Doctors, Dentists, therapists, teachers, etc. One important and often overlooked is that if the children don't have a therapist, it is wise to have one available. These are especially traumatic times for kids.

Normalcy is an aid to transition. Remember this event is not only thrust on you but it is also thrust on these kids as well. Since most times the Grandparents don't live in the same school district the kids will have to change schools. To soften that blow, if possible, shuttle them back and forth to at least some of their old familiar friends, after school programs, sports teams, etc. If that is not possible seek out like kind programs to enroll them in that speak to their interests. No matter how difficult this becomes it will go a long way to softening the blow of all the chaos.

Another source of normalcy may be to ask the kids what kinds of things they did at home. Things like game night, movie night, trips to the park, Christmas or other holiday rituals, birthday parties, etc. Facilitate them staying in touch with their best friend if appropriate or possible. Familiar family gatherings of Aunts, Uncles, cousins will help. You can't duplicate everything but if you can, you will contribute to their adjustment to the new normal.

It is important that you address things like discipline, house rules and boundaries. Be aware most kids will take these early on. Your secret weapon is consistency sprinkled with a bit of compassion.

Support, support and some more support. Seek out support from family, church community, social service providers, neighbors, friends or anyone that makes this part of the journey easier. In the first two sentences when I repeated support several times it was not just for emphasis. You will need all kinds of support for the kids as well as for yourselves. You may also need financial help to make this work. You may need support from your workplace to take some time off for appointments, etc.

One consideration that is most overlooked is self-care. Let me be succinct here, "If the caregiver doesn't survive there is no care." Keep your finger on your own pulse while you are busy stepping up to a huge responsibility that was not your own doing. Let yourself feel all the feelings. As my friend Greg Payne (Cool Grandpa) says, "Give your Grandparenting self some Grace." Get help from a professional or local support group whenever appropriate. If you are a couple this goes double for your spousal relationship. This will be a great strain on everyone and difficult to adjust to. It is not only OK but essential that you tend to your needs regularly and quickly.

Just to drive this point home a bit more there are quite a few common concerns and challenges that Grandparents caring for their Grandchildren have. Some of these concerns may surprise you. Let's just browse the list.

Your own health and sense of wellbeing WILL be tested. Your relationship with your spouse WILL be tested. Some of the obvious stressors are things like the challenges of finances, disappointment, sudden quickening of activities, more demands on your energy, fear of the unknown, etc. In addition to these you may be experiencing things like; A change in your social circles. Many Grandparents actually have to move if they live in an adult community or a small condo that is not large enough to accommodate this new family. Children aren't a part of many of Grandparents' usual activities. You may not have time for that golf game or that Bridge tournament anymore. Many Grandparents express that their friends fade away for unexplained reasons. The term for this is Social Isolation.

One biggy is dealing with the emotionally driven behaviors that show up in children after such a trauma as this. This huge change seldom escapes acting out. This goes back to the support component of what you will need. Most Grandchildren react poorly to this abandonment and that may manifest in all kinds of behavior that doesn't seem to make sense to anyone much less a Grandparent that is in the swamp trying to do all they can for this child. Many Grandparents, at first, see this as ingratitude. The truth is that this is real to that child and, often with professional help, you are their only hope to weather this storm in their lives. Please listen to me when I say that this is not one of those things you want that child to push down and ignore. Just look at your own feeling of disappointment and multiply that considerably. It is paramount that you deal with this.

I am sure your values of discipline in your home may be different from what your Grandkids are used to. I would like to suggest that you consider these necessary discussions with your Grandchildren with a sprinkling of compassion. I am not suggesting they get a free pass. I am suggesting that this change will be hard for them as well as you. This is one area that you will be called upon to be very creative. Some Grandparents have gotten help in this area by talking with teachers, school counselors, therapists, etc. This is one of those responsibilities that falls on you to be true to yourself and as considerate to the Grandchild as possible. I liken it to a high wire act at the circus. Good Luck.

Combining these last two concerns with the idea of considerable generational differences will produce its own set of challenges. This requires learning and empathy. On the heels of all this change we will be well served to understand that we may not even be speaking the generational language our young Grandchildren understand. This is as foreign to them as it is to us. I still use the word "cool". How's that for a generational gap in language?

One of the nagging details of raising your Grandchildren is putting in place a plan that will take care of them when you can no longer be the caregiver. Your health or financial resources may not stretch far enough. Then what? Planning for the long-term care of the entire, now expanded, family is different from what you had before the kids arrived on your doorstep. You have had your retirement interrupted already. One or both of you may need to return to the workforce to make this work.

Chapter 4

RESOURCES

AARP Grandfamilies Guide
https://www.aarp.org/relationships/friends-family/info-08-2011/grandfamilies-guide-support.html

This resource is a window into all the considerations and how to get help in those areas.

Generations United
https://www.gu.org/

This is one of the first organizations and they are part of all of the resources that exist. They advocate for children.

The mission of Generations United is to improve the lives of children, youth, and older people through intergenerational collaboration, public policies, and programs for the enduring benefit of all.

Grandfamilies.org
https://www.grandfamilies.org/State-Fact-Sheets

This is the repository for a state-by-state listing of Grand facts. This is a living document and is updated regularly by the leading Grandparent Organizations in the US. Here you will find the best information state by state, which is important because laws, etc., change from state to state and apply in the state the child is residing. This site is offered in English and Spanish.

Facebook Groups

Facebook has a support group for everyone. This is especially true for Grandparents. I caution you to do your homework. Some of these groups get a bit dicey.

HelpGuide.org
https://www.helpguide.org

This site offers some really good ideas and support for the Grandparents that are raising these Grandchildren.

HelpGuide.org is an independent nonprofit that runs one of the world's leading mental health websites. Each month, millions of people from all around the world turn to us for trustworthy information they can use to improve their mental health and make healthy changes.

National Committee of Grandparents for Children's Rights
https://ncrc.org

Over 2.6 million children in the United States are being raised by grandparents, other relatives or close family friends. While it can be extremely rewarding for an older adult to take on the responsibility of raising a child, there are also many challenges that arise. There is a wide variety of reasons kinship families' form. However, regardless of how they come together, many of them face similar difficulties such as navigating the welfare system, establishing legal guardianship and moving past trauma. NCRC created this database of resources for grandfamilies to help provide support and assistance for older adults caring for children.

Parents Helping Parents (A virtual Support Group)
https://parentshelpingparents.org/grandparents-as-caregivers

Parents Helping Parents (PHP) prevention philosophy is grounded in a self-help model based on the belief that parents can develop their own solutions when given the space, encouragement, and community resources that they need. Thus, it is the parents themselves who decide the direction a conversation will take during a Parent Support Group meeting or call our Parent Stress Line.

BenefitsCheckUp
https://benefitscheckup.org/

BenefitsCheckUp® is the nation's most comprehensive online tool to connect older adults and people with disabilities to benefit assistance. We'll make it easy to see if you may be eligible—and then help you find out where to apply online or how to get help from a benefits counselor.

BenefitsCheckUp helps assess whether you can get help from programs before you apply. Answer questions anonymously to find out if you may be eligible for key benefits assistance, including the Supplemental Nutrition Assistance Program (SNAP), Medicare Savings Programs, Medicaid, Medicare Part D Low Income Subsidy (LIS) - Extra Help, among others.

State Temporary Assistance for Needy Families (TANF)
https://www.benefits.gov/benefit/613

This is a resource for the short-term needs of a family in crisis. The Temporary Assistance for Needy Families (TANF) program provides grant funds to states and territories to provide families with financial assistance and related support services. State-administered programs may include childcare assistance, job preparation, and work assistance.

Earned Income Tax Credit and Child Tax Credit
https://www.irs.gov/credits-deductions/individuals

The Earned Income Tax Credit and the Child Tax Credit are both programs designed to help alleviate poverty, but there are key differences. The EITC is a credit available to employed, low-income households. It is intended to boost the effective income of people who are employed. The CTC is a credit available to employed households with children. This credit is intended to help offset the costs of raising children. Both can be very valuable for qualifying taxpayers.